CW01483741

TRACKING
THE
BLACK DOG

TRACKING
THE
BLACK DOG

HAIRY TALES AND HISTORICAL
LEGWORK FROM THE BLACK DOG
INSTITUTE'S WRITING COMPETITION

Edited by KERRIE EYERS

UNSW
PRESS

BLACK DOG INSTITUTE

A UNSW Press book

Published by
University of New South Wales Press Ltd
University of New South Wales
Sydney NSW 2052
AUSTRALIA
www.unswpress.com.au

in association with
Black Dog Institute
Prince of Wales Hospital
Randwick NSW 2031

For more about the Writing Competition and the Black Dog
Institute please visit www.blackdoginstitute.org.au

© Black Dog Institute 2006
First published 2006, Reprinted 2006

This book is copyright. Apart from any fair dealing for the purpose
of private study, research, criticism or review, as permitted under the
Copyright Act, no part may be reproduced by any process without
written permission. Inquiries should be addressed to the publisher.

National Library of Australia
Cataloguing-in-Publication entry
  Tracking the black dog: hairy tales and historical
  legwork from the Black Dog Institute's Writing Competition.

  ISBN 0 86840 812 3.
  1. Depression, Mental. I. Eyers, Kerrie.

  616.8527

Design Di Quick
Cover illustration Matthew Johnstone,
  author of *I Had a Black Dog* (Pan Macmillan, 2005).
Print Griffin Press

All reasonable efforts were taken to obtain permission to use copyright material reproduced in this book, but in some cases copyright
holders could not be traced. The publishers welcome information in
this regard.

A RESPECTFUL DEDICATION TO A STATESMAN

SIR WINSTON CHURCHILL

The Right Honourable Sir Winston Leonard
Spencer-Churchill, KG, OM, CH, FRS, PC
30 November 1874 – 24 January 1965

The Spencer-Churchill's family motto was *fiel pero desdichado*, which can be translated from the Spanish as 'faithful but unfortunate': concordant with Winston Churchill's affliction, for Churchill struggled with depression, as did many of his ancestors, the Dukes of Marlborough. He called it his 'black dog', and while Churchill was not the first person to so describe his depressive episodes, he certainly popularised the term.

His courage in dealing with his recurrent and prolonged depressive episodes was inspirational. He said: 'Courage is the first of human qualities because it is the quality which guarantees all others.'

He was, in addition to his many other talents, a witty and a scholarly man, and the 1953 Nobel Prize laureate in literature. His legacy provides a distinguished backdrop against which to display the following excerpts from our writers, with their mix of careful research, personal insights and, sometimes black, humour.

CONTENTS

CONTENTS

The Black Dog Institute – providing clinical and research expertise, education and training, and community support – is dedicated to improving the understanding, diagnosis and treatment of depression and bipolar disorder. The Institute, incorporating the clinical research Mood Disorders Unit, was launched in 2002.

Black Dog! How did the Institute get its name? Sir Winston Churchill used this term to describe his own depression. Accordingly, the Institute logo has Churchill's V for Victory in the foreground casting the shadow of a dog, which respects the reality that, while depression can be beaten, it still shadows the sufferer.

The inaugural Black Dog Institute Writing Competition reflected the Institute's interest in tracing the origins of the term 'black dog' as used to describe depression. The challenge was to investigate the meaning and the roots of the phrase.

FOREWORD

Professor Gordon Parker has honoured me by requesting that I write a short foreword for this book. That said, I could not help being reminded of advice given by one of my teachers, Max Hamilton, that I should rue the day when colleagues start asking for prefaces rather than more substantial pieces!

As often happens with books on melancholia and germane subjects, this charming compilation says more about its scholarly contributors than about the theme itself, which I take to be the historical and cultural link between the 'black dog' metaphor, the old concept of melancholia and the clusters of feelings and behaviours nowadays called 'disorders of the affect'. In other words, the issue in hand is not the history of the metaphorical usage of 'black dog' itself or the clinical vicissitudes of Winston Churchill, but the moment when such metaphoric usage became firmly linked to at least one of the acceptions of melancholia.

Unfortunately, the term melancholia remains chained to a rather unintelligible etymology. For can the 'black bile' concept tell anything meaningful to the modern person? Whether psychiatrist or not, can he/she even begin to understand the meaning of a referent constructed in a world of ideas which is now remote and alien? How does the modern person then conceive of 'black bile'? Might it be just like bile only that it is 'black'? As a different kind of fluid? Perchance, as something other than a fluid? Has the Greek stem μελαζ – *melas* – anything to do with the colour black as conceived of in the twenty-first century? After all, the Greeks used the same adjective to refer to red wine, the heart of oak, and metaphorically to enigmatic persons. When calling black bile black, were they 'seeing' (or perhaps 'conceiving of') it as black? Or perhaps as red, obscure, inscrutable?

The answer is that we shall never know, because the ontology and epistemology (that is, its nature and means to know it) of 'black bile' were part and parcel of a particular and integrated metaphysical conception of the world, and that world has now gone forever. The 'black bile' cannot be torn away from the Greek model of the world and just grafted onto the current episteme. The fact that we can do that with horses or with the mount Olympus creates an epistemological mirage. It would be a categorical mistake, however, to consider black bile as a natural kind. It was just an abstract organisational concept which evaporated together with the panoply of ideas that the Greeks created to organise their world.

By the same token, we know little about what the Greeks did mean by melancholia. Classicists tell us that the referent of the word included conditions such as malaria, paralysis and some strange behaviours and appearances difficult for us to categorise but which had little to do with what is called a 'major depressive episode with melancholic features' in DSM-IV. Indeed, because they belong in parallel conceptual universes, the DSM meaning of melancholia and its Greek homonym can be considered as incommensurable in Kuhn's sense of the term.

If so, how come that people still write books on the history of melancholia and depression 'from the Greeks to the present'? Why do people persist with the rather silly claim that it was

Aretæus of Cappadocia who 'discovered' bipolar disorder? These questions have clear answers, but it is prudent to pass them in silence. Suffice to say that such books are biographies of words pretending to be histories of natural kinds or nosological entities.

We also know that the scaffolding supporting the current notions of affective disorder, depression and melancholia, was constructed only during the nineteenth century. It was during this period that the mandarins of the discipline decided on new names and classifications for the 'primary' functions of the mind, and fractured madness along putative new planes of cleavage. This is how depression and mania became 'primary disorders' of emotions, mood, and affect. The twentieth century froze these 'disorders' into 'operational definitions' and itemised their components into 'measuring' instruments. The control that these conceptual filters have on the clinical gaze explains why researchers regularly 'confirm' that the affective disorders are exactly what they are (no more, no less). Finding their aetiology and the magic bullet are now more important objectives than calling into question their shape, boundaries and psychopathological content.

Parallel to this 'medical' tradition, the scholar will also find in the cultures of the West a 'literary' tradition featuring mood states such as melancholy, wistfulness, mournful expectancy, lover's malady, and its accompanying polyphony of sighs, whimpers, and soft rustling sounds. This tradition cannot be traced back beyond the early medieval period, and its relationship to the medical tradition remains something of a mystery. Much as one may wish to assume that the medical and literary traditions borrowed from each other, crucial research on this theme is still needed. More quoted than read, Robert Burton was able to differentiate them and, for all his 'medical' training, he could only bequeath to us an ambiguous definition of melancholia.

Lawrence Bab, a great historian of the literary tradition, was also able to differentiate between the 'lover's malady' and mental disorders; and so did Panofsky and Saxl in 1923.

Given this historical elusiveness, it is not an easy task to identify the moment when the 'black dog' metaphor became attached to one of the concepts comprised in the melancholia story. Since human creativity works at its best in the chiaroscuro, asking the question was a good idea in the first place. The rich pickings collected in this book not only confirm that this is the case but also support the belief that psychiatric questions are better dealt with when answers are sought outside the medical model.

Professor German Berrios
Reader in the Epistemology of Psychiatry
University of Cambridge

ACKNOWLEDGMENTS

First, a meaty bone for the Director of the Black Dog Institute, Professor Gordon Parker, whose curiosity about the phrase 'black dog' led to his suggestion of em-barking on the Black Dog Writing Competition – now an annual event.

Next our warm appreciation to two generous and distinguished professionals, my co-judges John Gascoigne and Judy Washington, who were immersed for three weeks in the flood of truly inspirational entries.

Recognition to the ever-gracious Sue Grdovic, project manager for Consumer and Community Programs, for shaping and managing the competition so competently, and to Ian Dose, the Institute's public relations guru – who maintains a modest near-invisibility while propelling the Institute to ever greater heights.

A madrigal for Tessa Wigney, community liaison officer, who spent much time 'dog wrangling' but retained her sunny good humour, and a sonnet for Pauline Trantalis, who so ably supports every facet of the Institute, all backed, as usual, by Christine Boyd, our indispensable facilities manager.

Many thanks to creative artists David Frazer and Matthew Johnstone. David kindly allowed us to use his beautifully evocative images of 'joyful sadness'. Matthew Johnstone, author of the luminous book *I Had a Black Dog*, created the artwork for the cover and, generous as ever, allowed us to kennel a few more black hounds in the book.

The illustrations on pages 54 and 67 are reprinted with permission from Janet and Colin Bord from their 1980 book *Alien Animals: A Worldwide Investigation*, Grenada, London, and the Fortean Picture Library, Henblas, Mwrog Street, Ruthin, LL15 1LG, UK.

Paul Foley's winning essay is framed by lyrics from the song *Black Dog*, words and music by Chris O'Doherty, copyright Syray Music/Universal Music Publishing P/L (all rights reserved), reprinted with permission.

Quotations from works by Les Murray (pages 114–115 and 137) and Peter Brown (peterxbrown, page 116) are included with permission.

PASTORAL MELANCHOLY – DAVID FRAZER

PREFACE

The Black Dog Institute is a clinical, research and educational body with a strong community focus dedicated to improving the understanding, diagnosis and treatment of the depressive and bipolar disorders. The Institute was formally launched in 2002, incorporating its clinical research predecessor, the Mood Disorders Unit.

The Institute's name reflects Sir Winston Churchill's description of his own depression – the 'black dog'. Our logo has Churchill's 'V' for victory in the foreground, but casting the shadow of a dog, respecting the reality that, while depression can be mastered, it still shadows the sufferer.

We knew that Churchill was not the first to describe the 'black dog': the metaphor goes back to Celtic times, when those developing depression described a 'black dog' or a 'black fog' enveloping them. The history of the metaphor was also foggy, and the Institute therefore launched an essay competition in 2004 to pursue the meaning and the roots of the phrase 'black dog'. The challenge was enthusiastically taken up by nearly three hundred writers, and our judges (Kerrie Eyers, John Gascoigne and Judy Washington) were captivated by the high quality and richness of the essays.

It seemed imperative to conserve both the historical

research and the tenor of the essays by preserving excerpts from many of them, as well as publishing the three prize-winning essays in full. Kerrie Eyers, the Institute's publications consultant, was commissioned to tackle the complex task, and has ensured that key historical points were captured and redundancy avoided, while interleaving historical and psychiatric nuances with a light hand and luminous whimsy.

The whole is truly greater than the sum of the parts, and a splendid tapestry is now observable, with the richness of the 'black dog' metaphor and its history collected in this anthology. Paul Foley, first-prize winner, observes that the combination of blackness and dog provides an eminent description of depression; an ever-present companion, lurking just out of sight, vaguely menacing, capable of overwhelming at any moment. David Musgrave notes the paradox: 'the dog is valuable to us because it retains many of the characteristics of the wolf from which it is descended ... The deep familiarity of the dog to the human sits alongside that part of its nature which is unfamiliar and alien'.

Megan McKinlay brings the prominence of the metaphor back to Churchill. 'It is because of who Churchill was, the particular way in which he returned the black dog to popular consciousness, that it evolved into the symbol that we have today ... He recognised his own suffering in it, and adopted it, and because of his public profile and the unique circumstances of his life, added dimensions to the metaphor that gave it a broader appeal.' Thus, an iteration between a mood state, a metaphor and a man.

Professor German Berrios of Cambridge University, in his erudite and multilayered foreword, has illuminated many of the threads in the ancient tapestry of ascriptions leading to our topic. We continue to weave our own metaphors into any new awareness, but we can never truly comprehend the earlier patterns. As LP Hartley said, 'The past is a foreign country, they do things differently there'. This endeavour, though, has teased out a thread that runs from then through now – understanding and healing disorders of the mind and emotions must respect the arts as much as the sciences. May you therefore enjoy the historical intrigue captured here in tracking the history of the black dog. It's a story that resonates with our institute's motto – 'To advance we must understand; to understand we must advance'.

Professor Gordon Parker
Executive Director
Black Dog Institute

HAIRY TALES AND HISTORICAL LEGWORK

Outside of a dog, a book is man's best friend.
Inside of a dog it's too dark to read.
Groucho Marx

The following compilation consists of gems forged from individuals' research and imagination and threaded together by the common theme. Each writer turns a different facet of the topic to the light: a collage of gods and dogs, lyrical archetypes and black superstition, and terrifying or soothing beliefs in the setting of an indifferent cosmos …

THE START
OF THE TAIL

Dogs, I have found in my reading, suffer from depression too, and respond well to Prozac and other drugs – whether it's merely kennel cough that's getting them down, or being the subject of investigative essays about their fiendish proclivities. JEFFREY

Always ... dogs have doggedly dogged humans, while themselves for the most part leading dogs' lives. It may sound trite, but it is also true, that it is by the very reason of dogs' unique propensity to follow relentlessly that dog-ged as an adjective, and dogged, as a verb, have acquired the very meanings they have. So we have terms like 'dogged by bad luck' and 'dog-ged pursuit' (which actually compliment the dog's determined nature, notwithstanding the unpleasantness or onerous implications of the terms themselves). Dogs are good at, and good for, being dog-ged, even though humans hate being dogged. BRUCE

You will be familiar with the saying 'life's a bitch and then you die' – well, here are some more words to describe my character – 'go to the dogs', 'lame dog', 'dog box', 'dog-eared', 'dogfight', 'dogged', 'doggie bag' (leftover food often spiked with MSG), 'doghouse', 'dog in the manger', 'dog-tired', 'dogsbody', 'dog's breakfast', 'dogwatch'. There is 'mongrel', 'bitch', 'cur', 'Kerr's Cur', and I could continue but instead I will let sleeping dogs lie (and humans lie sleepless). JOAN

Regarding the word 'dog' it is worth considering its past and present usage: a black dog used to be thought unlucky; dogs are supposed to howl at the time of someone's death; dogs possess the ability to see ghosts; a dog's life is one that is never left in peace; to go to the dogs is to go to rack and ruin; to die like a dog is to have a miserable end; the dogs of war are the horrors of armed conflict – and an individual's hangdog expression means guilt, shamefaced and/or dejected. On top of this, rabid dogs added yet more to traditional beliefs: the fear of being bitten and as a consequence, suffering a painful death and insanity. FRED

In modern parlance, we let sleeping dogs lie; we go to the dogs or die like a dog; we dog someone at every turn, or compete in a dog-eat-dog environment. And when we put a name to our depression, increasingly it is that of the black dog, lurking behind us, or clinging tenaciously to our backs. The statesman and politician Winston Churchill drew upon this image to conceptualise his own struggle with depression, and it is with him that the metaphor is generally associated. Indeed, so firmly linked are the man and the image in contemporary usage that some references make the man an integral part of the metaphor. MEGAN

First impressions of the chase

Whoever dreamed up this essay should take a bow. Wow! As dogged as I've been by attacks of depression ever since I was just a pup, and as sick as I've grown of hearing myself whining about my symptoms – sadness, anger, anxiety, agitation, insomnia, lassitude, loss of appetite for food, society and sex and so on – this challenge really has me pricking up my ears. I know, I know, irrational elation is just another side of the syndrome. But as thoroughly as I should have trained myself by now not to jerk my own chain by getting my hopes too high, I just can't help hoping at times that if I only beg hard enough, or dig in just the right spot, fate may yet throw me a bone. DEAN

Although I found this topic drier than a bone at the outset I challenged myself to grab it by the scruff and get on with the job. What began as a dog-day afternoon, when I was coming out of my last depressive bout for 2004, has become, for me, a fascinating shaggy dog tale. I have worked liked a dog, hounded down numerous texts, articles, countless references and trivial titbits,

ANOTHER NIGHT ON EARTH – DAVID **FRAZER**

personal views from the Internet, and extended my own frames of reference. I have created from my own 20-year experience with bipolar disorder an almost lovable Black Wolfhound ... To proceed! Every dog has its day in this dog-eat-dog world and one has to be in it to win. So I will go fetch. GILLIAN

It was never a dog for me. I admire Winston Churchill, and he would have liked me, too – I can tell by the sparkle in his eye. I can understand, too, why it was a dog for him. He's English, after all, and dogs have been close companions to the English for a long time now. But my depression was something more nebulous than a dog, though it was black, the colour in which hope and joy have vanished. If I could liken it at all to an object, it was a black cloud hanging behind my head. It wasn't always present, but when it was, it hung behind me no matter which way I turned. It could not be dislodged, and it could fold silently around me and hold me powerless. It was something – as the Black Dog Institute's web pages say – that there was no 'capacity to resist'. BERNADETTE

It is just as well that there is no fun in research anymore (as 'all ye know on earth, and all ye need to know' is only a mouse-click away), because we depressives, 'we few, we happy few, we band of brothers', find no fun in anything any more, and for a long time before that ... looking at the worst-case scenario (as we do) for the rest of our 'solitary, poor, nasty, brutish and short' lives. Indeed, if this topic had to be researched in the old-fashioned way the august setters of this Essay Competition would not have many entries to judge, and they only from depressives who, lucky bastards, have the occasional manic phase. The rest of us, being too afraid, or tired, or disorganised or, er, depressed to brave buses, and libraries, and librarians, and Members of the Public, and every vexing, miserable new hell that awaits Out There, much prefer the solitary pleasures of the Internet. GRAHAM

Hair of the (black) dog

I myself had a little black dog, twenty-some years ago, a kelpie-cross named Sam. He was not the Black Dog of Depression, on the contrary, he was a gracious, grateful, brave little friend always; simple pleasures were plenty for him, and he had only one bad habit: everywhere he lay became coated with darkness, as a layer of his jet-black hair accumulated there. Such places became progressively duller, dimmer, depressing-looking; Sam's corner of the room, and his spot in my car, always looked as though the sun never shone there. Everyone who has kept a real live black dog will testify to the truth of what I am saying. The huge black long-haired dogs, such as those bred for hunting bears in cold northern European countries, must darken whole rooms with their hair, especially in spring when they moult. BRUCE

Fangs for the memory

Last Christmas while visiting my parents-in-law's farm on the western plains of New South Wales, I was bitten by Oscar, one of my father-in-law's dogs. It was a cheeky little nip on the ankle that failed to draw blood and earned him a smack and a scolding, but didn't stop him from repeating the offence a number of times over the week we were there. Quite some time later I discovered that Oscar did not belong to the family of dogs born and bred on the farm ... He had been sent to them through the agency of a friend in Sydney because of a number of behavioural problems which made it impossible for his Sydney owners to keep him. One of those misdemeanours was to bite the visiting former US president Bill Clinton one morning as he took an early morning stroll somewhere in Rushcutters Bay. Naturally, my first reaction on learning this was immense pride, knowing that I had been bitten by the same dog that had bitten an American president. For a while, my boasting knew no bounds: apart from being a pair of charismatic devils, Bill Clinton and I had something else in common. DAVID

WHAT'S IT ALL ABOUT?

Homo sapiens has a very innovative side ... he solves problems by inventing 'tools', is creative in regard to language and the other arts. As long as he has a mission to fulfil he feels contented with his life up to a point. Above all he is superstitious and tends to anthropomorphise. But when in a rut the innate loneliness and insignificance of his existence manifests. ROSLYN

To anthropomorphise is to consider any non-human thing as if it has human characteristics and try to interact with it accordingly.

So human an animal

Psychologist Abraham Maslow (1908–1970) conceived the idea of a hierarchy of human needs. Once pressing biological demands for food, water and shelter are satisfied, the need for security is the next to become active; after that, love and a sense of belonging, followed by the quest for self-esteem and the esteem of others. If all these needs are satisfied, then the individual can pursue self-actualisation: being or doing what that person was born to be, or do.

Thus humans seek to make sense of, gain control over and give meaning to their lives and their environment. Myths capture age-old themes and stories that recur as human dilemmas; rituals are devised to appease and to console; metaphor diffuses meaning to a more symbolic level; and, when all else fails, superstition and prejudice provide a sense of inclusion.

Myth, archetype and metaphor

The best allegories, the ones which stand the test of time because of the truth they seem to express so aptly, become myths, proverbs, folktales and even clichés. It is through allegorical stories that a culture stores its accumulated wisdoms ... the Book of Proverbs, Aesop's Fables ... They are familiar because they are often repeated, and they are often repeated because they seem to embody something we recognise as the truth ... When Winston Churchill famously described his fits of depression as being 'a black dog' that hounded him, he was not inventing a wholly new expression, but choosing a metaphor that, maybe unconsciously, felt right to him ... The archetypal black dog has world-wide parallels, appearing and reappearing in such similar guises that we can only agree with the mythology scholar Joseph Campbell when he remarks: 'The themes are timeless, and the inflection is in the culture'.[1] CATE

Myths are

> an arrangement of the past, whether real or imagined, in patterns that reinforce a culture's deepest values and aspirations ... They are the maps by which cultures navigate through time.[2]

Archetypes are ancient, but the concept is preserved in Jungian psychology which holds that humans share a collective unconscious so that each inherits the recognition of patterns of thought or symbolic imagery derived from the past collective experience, hence the recurrence of such symbols and metaphors.

Metaphor is closely related to simile (x is 'like' y). Metaphor (x *is* y) directly identifies one object or idea with another, in one or more aspects: it expands the sense and clarifies the meaning, drawing a parallel between concepts. For instance, 'he's a real pussycat' said about an acquaintance indicates that he's a human who is (a) not as fierce as he seems and/or (b) a bit of a pushover.

> Even today we are shocked and horribly fascinated when some beloved pet turns on his owner or neighbour, or when a dingo, so very close in appearance to the playful dog down the street, steals a baby from a tent. We humanise dogs, expect better of them – conveniently forgetting our own occasional ferocious behaviour. The dog is, after all, the same lovable creature that guides blind people and plays with toddlers, so it is doubly horrific when a member of that breed becomes a ferocious attacker. ALLAN

The historical portrayal and perception of the dog, especially in terms of its relationship with human beings, has

... vacillated between that of companion, healer, funerary aid and supernatural threat, with the latter assumption tending to dominate. Whilst this may seem odd in light of the common western appeal of pet ownership, it strikes a more understandable chord when we consider the dog in symbolic terms, '[existing] precariously in the no-man's land between the human and non-human worlds ... an interstitial creature, neither person nor beast, forever oscillating uncomfortably between the roles of high-status animal and low-status person.'[3] Whilst this harks back to the human/canine parallel outlined in the ... pre-Islamic myths ... the dog throughout much of history has still come off second best and been transformed into 'a creature of metaphor, simultaneously embodying or representing a strange mixture of admirable and despicable traits.'[4] MARTINE

The dog and man have a long and complex history of interaction, full of ambivalent and contradictory significations. Both classical and contemporary iconography and symbology – as represented in art, literature, popular culture and the images of ancient mythologies – feature a myriad of canine incarnations, figures whose presence resonates with a significance beyond the contours of their physical form. In the competing and complementary representations of classical mythology, dogs menace, defile, and patrol borders, both earthly and supernatural, but also heal, protect, purify, and act as symbols of loyalty and fidelity. MEGAN

'Black dog' is a powerfully expressive metaphor that appears to require no explanation. The combination of blackness with the negative connotations of 'dog', noun and verb, seems an eminently apt description of depression: an ever-present companion, lurking in the shadows just out of sight, growling, vaguely menacing, always on the alert; sinister and unpredictable, capable of overwhelming you at any moment. Further, the dark hound is an archetypal object of fear, with a long tradition in folklore and myth. Black dogs in dreams are interpreted negatively, often representing death; from all over the world come tales of nightmares caused by oppressive black dogs crushing the sleeper's chest. PAUL

Black, the old blue

The symbolism of colours was established early in human history. Black is the absence of all colour, the shade of night, storm clouds, animals' lairs, closed eyes and rotting wounds. It was first associated with sorrow, fear, death, famine, mourning and injury. As spiritualism developed, societies associated black with evil, sin and Hell ... Ancient Greek and Roman writers ... refer to the symbolism of the colour black ... An excess of black bile was thought to be the cause of melancholia, providing a medical link between black and despair. CHRIS

Darkness has always been cursed, not only for the fact that it so paralyses human activity, but also because Darkness and Evil are everywhere seen as blood brothers. It is the necessary corollary of God's seeing that the Light was Good. Blackness, from antiquity, from the very beginning in fact, has universally symbolised ignorance, despair, grief, evil and Death itself. BRUCE

[21]

Black clothing is a sign of mourning going back to the Egyptians and copied by the Romans. The Latin word *niger* for black also means bad or unpropitious. Black oxen were sacrificed to Pluto (the Roman ruler of the underworld) and other deities connected with the infernal regions ... in the *Oxford Universal Dictionary* ... there is reference to 'the Black Book – an official return prepared in the reign of Henry VIII containing the abuses in the monasteries.' A black sheep in the flock was once regarded as having the Devil's mark, and the metaphorical term for a disgraced member of a family or community is a black sheep. Muslims say that the famous black stone at Mecca was once white when it fell from heaven but turned black because of the sins of mankind. LOIS

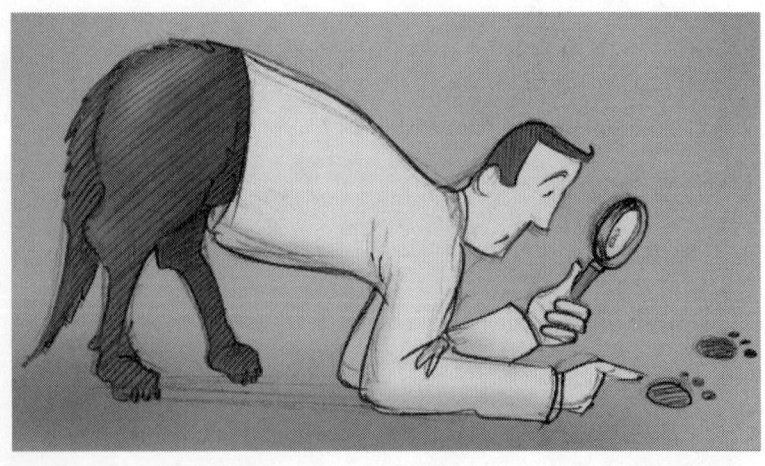

– MATTHEW JOHNSTONE

Black is one of the more commonly used colours in [the Bible], used to describe the colour of the middle of the night (Proverbs 7:9); diseased skin (Job 30:30); ... corpses' faces (Lamentations 4:8); trouble (Job 3:5); the darkening of the sun and the moon (Joel 2:10). In Taoist philosophy, *yin* signifies blackness, mystery, emotion, death and emptiness ... REBECCA

In western culture, the colour black continues down the centuries to have symbolic meaning. In art it denotes evil, falsehood and error. In the Christian church, black decoration has been used for Good Friday, and as a mortuary colour signifying grief, despair and death. Mutes who wore black coats followed the coffin at funerals. MARY

DIGGING FOR THE PHRASE

May I ... put forward for your consideration: melas (μελας), black + collie, a dog = melancholy = Black Dog. QED. GRAHAM

Some older phrases describing melancholy, such as the *mumblefubbles*, have fallen out of use.[5] SUZANNE

[In exploring the history of the term Black Dog] ... we are faced with a three-pronged puzzle that involves the words 'black', 'dog' and 'depression'. Each has a history of its own and is infused with layers of meaning. The challenge is to peel back those individual layers, in order to unveil how the influence of particular cultural beliefs and approaches has left indelible marks on the language in question and fed our need to qualify experience through metaphor. MARTINE

It is worthwhile trying to pinpoint the moment when the term 'black dog' entered into English as a specific description of depression: this has as much to do with the evolution of the term 'depression', in distinction from the earlier, more encompassing term 'melancholy', as it does with a sudden shift of the usage of 'black dog' as a figure of folklore to a figure of personalised, psychological description.

The dog is a companion, man's best friend as the cliché goes. As an object of affectional touch and hugging, the dog serves basic human emotional needs. But, paradoxically, the dog is valuable to us because it retains many of the characteristics of the wolf from which it is descended: a distrust of strangers and a marked territorialism (making it an ideal guardian of self and property); the ability to herd and hunt. Yet, for all that, a dog can bite (and does). The deep familiarity of the dog to the human sits alongside that part of its nature which is unfamiliar and alien, and it is the uneasy co-existence of these qualities that is the genesis for the term 'black dog'. DAVID

Why is 'black dog' ultimately such a popular term? Perhaps because it reflects a certain attitude to the experience of depression: it externalises the dark feelings as a companion, albeit an unwelcome companion; it expresses some of the oppression not heard in 'depression' … it emphasises, in contrast to earlier romantic–intellectual interpretations of melancholia, that depression may be distinct from the underlying personality. In this sense, it is a metaphor of hope: the black dog may be to some extent a friend, but he is a bad friend; and as with anyone who renders life miserable and restricts interactions and possibilities, he needs to be left behind, no matter how persistent his pursuit. PAUL

GOOD DOG, BAD DOG

Homer, in Book 17 of the *Odyssey*, describes 'Argos, the hound of Odysseus, of the steadfast heart'. Odysseus had bred and raised Argos himself, but 'had no joy of him' because he had to go and fight in the Trojan War. Argos had been a magnificent dog; people

> would be amazed at seeing his speed and his strength. No creature that he started at in the depths of the thick wood could escape him, and in tracking too he was keen of scent.

As time went by and Odysseus did not return, Argos was neglected, and was finally cast out by Odysseus' household slaves. Homer recounts their reunion after twenty years. Only Argos recognised his master, Odysseus, the disguised King of Ithaca:

> There the dog Argos lay in the dung, all covered with dog ticks. Now, as he perceived that Odysseus had come close to him, he wagged his tail, and laid both his ears back; only he now no longer had the strength to move any closer to his master, who ... secretly wiped a tear away ... The doom of dark death now closed over the dog, Argos, when, after nineteen years had gone by, he had seen Odysseus ... and he died content.[6]

The word 'dog' in itself is a fitting one in its several implications. The Greek word *kynicos* means doglike, not in the devoted sense but churlish and uncooperative. We derive the word 'cynic' from a similar Greek word and Latin *cynicus* meaning 'dog', with its distrustful, sneering connotations. The word 'cynosure' refers to a dog's tail, in Latin *synosura*. LOIS

DARK DOGS
OF THE
UNDERWORLD

Mythology ... is psychology, misread as cosmology, history, and biology. The folk tale is the primer of the picture-language of the soul. – Joseph Campbell, *The Hero with a Thousand Faces*

Dogs and death

The development of this tendency to equate the dog with death, the underworld and resurrection grew from human observation of particular social and cultural practices. In one sense, since dogs were known to bury and retrieve their bones, it has been speculated from archaeological evidence gained from the Early Neolithic period that they may well have been used by early man to destroy corpses. What's more, ancient society's belief in the notion that eating involved the consumption of a food's essence would imply that the dog's devouring of a body included its ingestion or removal of the 'soul'. Whilst this burial practice may seem macabre, the use of animal scavengers for the defleshing of bodies has long been a part of the funeral rites of such races as the Parsees in India and the Scottish of the Orkney islands. In Roman times, this practice of excarnation was not considered flattering, with dogs being used as executioners or given the corpses of those unworthy of decent burial rites. MARTINE

Dogs and deity
Pre-Dynastic Egypt – the Mesolithic, Neolithic and Bronze Ages (6000–3100 BC) ...

Hecate was thought to originate from the great tribal matriarch, Heq or Heket, who was a midwife (bringer forth of life) and the Great Triple Goddess ... also known as Mother Earth [and Mother of the gods], who gave birth to the Earth ... Her triple aspect was represented by the three ages of woman – the virgin, the mother and the crone. The goddess Hecate represented the crone ... and the dark side of the moon, and it is here we find the origins of the relationship between the Black Dog and depression ... In a literal sense she guarded the entrance to Hades, in her form as the Black Dog Cerberus. In a metaphorical sense she was responsible for stages of transformation [such as] 'lunacy' where people were said to become moonstruck and entered a state of confusion, stupor and stagnation ... This was a necessary stage of transformation ... when the old has ended and the new is not yet seen – and once experienced leads to the light of creative energy. The Romans concentrated more on the negative aspects of [the black dog] archetype without providing a balance or hope that this stage would invariably pass ... they used a more literal definition of death as the end of life ... LEIGH

Black puppy: Bau (wow)

From Mesopotamia, the cradle of civilization [5500–500 BC], the veneration of the dog was manifested through the Sumerian dog-headed goddess, Bau. Worship of the Egyptian god, Anubis … (although at times appearing as a cross between a dog and a jackal) can be traced back to Bau; however [Anubis] assumes a much more ethereal and frightening quality. [Dogs are now] the 'psychopomps, the guides on the paths to the Otherworld, the guardians of the liminal zone at the boundaries of the worlds.'[7] This association also appears in the Hindu epic the Mahabharata, and a range of shamanic practices from around the world. MARTINE

'Liminal' is a word describing the threshold at which we are aware of an event and have a physiological or a psychological response. 'Subliminal' (used particularly in psychology) refers to a stimulus that is below the threshold of conscious perception, something that we are not fully aware of but to which we respond unconsciously.

Dogs and divination

Astrology and astronomy, largely developed by the Babylonians, at this time were one and the same, a respected science for more than two thousand years. Astrological charts were used to predict the recurrence of seasons and celestial events by the positions and aspects of celestial bodies. Greek, Roman and Arab scholars and priests used such charts to forecast natural disasters, and extended them to divination of human affairs. Such divination attempted to foretell events by augury or supernatural agency, using prophecy – foretelling, soothsaying, fortune telling, or that sign of something coming, an omen. Divination could be accomplished by using arrows with certain markings, drawn at random, consulting images, examining the entrails of animals sacrificed, and in many other ways.

Contemporary signs of the zodiac bear Roman names. Dogs, wolves and jackals are frequent referents.

Divination was forbidden by both Jewish and Moslem law. However, exception was sometimes made in the scriptures, and God could make known His will by lot, dreams, divine appointment, and direct communication via prophets.

The first clues to [the black dog's] personal metamorphosis lie in the universe itself. Bright and gleaming, Sirius the Dog Star predates knowledge. Its portent in the ancient world was of hot summer months, a time of sickness and death in the area of the Nile River and the Mediterranean, the cradle of our own civilisation. The waxing and waning of the pale moon tracked the mysterious bloody cycles of a woman's body, and at its fullest, the round pock-marked Wolf Moon gave humanity a word for madness – lunacy. The Earth itself was deep and dark, descending endlessly and welcome only to those night creatures, yellow-eyed or sightless, who could endure the unrelenting blackness which absorbed the bodies of the dead. These were riddles which helped form early attitudes to wolf and dog. SUE

[In the astrology of the time] the black dog ... appears as an aspect of Saturn (black), particularly as Saturn aspects Mars (the Roman Mars corresponds to the Greek Ares, at the heels of whom goes the dog) or the moon (dog), or Mercury (the Greek Hermes, a psychopomp). [Certain aspects of these planets] may indicate impediments (Saturn) to action (Mars), to feeling (the moon) and to communication (Mercury). JENNIFER

Blue healers

The dog ... usually is the companion of healers ... in Phoenician iconography the dog accompanies Gaia, the Great Physician ... Associated with Aesculapius, the dog heals by rebirth into a new life; its fidelity survives death. JENNIFER

Sumerian dog-headed goddess Bau['s] ... role of healer is purported to have reflected the popular belief in the healing value of a dog's medicinal nature (its licking of sores). This respect for the dog as healer was integral to early Greek society, with the animal's flesh and blood used to ward off evil spirits, or cure such ailments as epilepsy, jaundice, intestinal and stomach disorders or even prevent itching and hair growth. MARTINE

As well as sacrificing dogs to the gods, Mediterranean and Middle Eastern people used them as 'scape-dogs' in healing and cleansing rituals. It was thought that by touching a person's body, dogs could absorb diseases and impurities. They licked wounds to prevent abscesses forming or were rubbed across a pregnant woman's belly to purify her and her child. Dogs were also killed after someone's birth, illness or death in order to clean and protect them, either in this life or the next. Frequently the dog used in these ceremonies was black. CHRIS

During the time of Hippocrates (460–377 BC) it was believed that dogs played a vital role in the detection of diseases. In the face of a mysterious illness, a dog would have close contact with the patient, then later be killed and examined. In other words, the dog became polluted so that the person might be 'cleansed'. CAROL

Dogs and disease

Many of the 'deadly' black dogs were said to cause their victims to be unable to speak – a classic symptom of rabies. The rabies virus causes constriction of the throat, preventing swallowing, which gives dogs the characteristic 'foaming at the mouth' look; but in humans can cause patients to lose their voice. Also, rabid animals go through an affectionate phase, in which even wild animals will seem tame, and a violent phase, in which [they] will even attack inanimate objects. In some of the 'black dog' folktales the hounds are said to be harmless if undisturbed, while others merely follow close at a person's heels, the fear of imminent attack being the source of terror. Both fit well with the affectionate phase of the disease. Finally, although rabies, which spreads directly along nerves, can take anywhere from hours to months to reach the brain, once it does so it causes encephalitis (basically a swelling of the brain), with death following in two to five days. MARK

A rabies vaccine was developed in 1885. Does anyone remember the 1957 film *Old Yeller*?

Folk remedies such as 'hair of the dog', which later became a hangover cure, date back to a much older, but ineffectual, treatment for dog bites that says to place the burnt hair of the dog that caused the bite on the wound. JULIE

Pliny offers preventative treatments against rabies for dogs, which include putting chicken dung in the dog's food for the thirty days when Sirius is shining. Columella thought that dogs could be rendered immune to rabies if their tails were docked in a certain way.

Dog plagues, and the corresponding threat of rabies, were ... known to have affected early societies. Within an Islamic context, this is what prompted a decree by the Prophet Mohammed ... 'The black dog is the Devil... Kill every one of them which is black of this single colour.' MARTINE

Of jackals, dogs and wolves

Bob Trubshaw claims that when Anubis mythology travelled to preclassical Greece, as there are no jackals, the wolf aptly fitted the role. A wolf-headed man, the prototype of werewolves of subsequent folk belief, was struck. Apollo was named Lykegenes, meaning 'born from the she-wolf' ... The wolf was Apollo's special animal and a fitting sacrificial victim to his worship, Trubshaw maintains.[8] GILLIAN

Egypt's jackal god: Anubis

I have walked through
The valley of the shadow of death
I have walked in the company of the Black Dog.

He has taken me through the cavern of sighs,
Up the mountains of unrealistic expectation
Down beyond the underground caves of despair.
from Black Dog II, ELAINE FRY

In Egyptian mythology, the jackal-headed god Anubis was a more benign guardian and escort to the world of after-life. [As God of the Embalming Chamber he made certain that the dead were assured of life after death.] One's soul need only be as light as a feather to escape the eternal darkness of the underworld. SUE

> Fear the weight of your heart as I lead you down to the
> chamber of reckoning, where Thoth stands with scales
> in hand and the feather of Truth. HARRIET

Anubis weighs the heart of the deceased against the feather of Ma'at, goddess of truth and justice. If the heart outweighs the feather, it has been made heavy with evil deeds and it will be given to Ammit, the god with the crocodile head, who will eat it, thus condemning the deceased to oblivion for eternity. If the feather outweighs the heart, the deceased will be presented before Osiris, the Black One, to join the afterlife.

From melancholia to worse

> The *Book of the Dead* – a collection of ancient Egyptian
> texts written between 2600 BC and 1350 BC – has
> references to depression. Horapollo [an Egyptian
> priest] … related the figure of the dog with the dispo-
> sition of melancholics in general. DALE

The texts in the Egyptian *Book of the Dead* suggest that the Egyptians never represented their Tuat as an underworld or hell in the ancient Greek or Judeo-Christian sense, but rather as a place of becoming, a place of transformation. By changing the Tuat to Hell, the churchmen, philosophers and writers in those early centuries also changed the role of the black dog. The association with the Otherworld had always been there, but as the nature of the Otherworld changed, so did the reputation of its guides and guardians. The association with darkness still existed, but no longer did the black dog guide people through; the black dog became synonymous with the darkness itself. To understand this more fully, consider the extraordinary transition that was happening in those early centuries, from the polytheistic mythologies of ancient Egypt and the Mediterranean to the monotheistic mythology of Christianity. The seasonal observations of the ancient Egyptian religion with participation in the cycles of death and rebirth was very different from the resurrectionist philosophy of the Judeo-Christian religious tradition. The ancient Egyptians, like most pre-industrial cultures of the world, dreamed a dream of eternally returning, a dream of renewable creative experience … From this perspective, the guardian of the Otherworld was not to be feared in the same way as a 'Hell' hound might be. HOLLY

The influence of monotheism

With the development of monotheistic religions, the dog's perceived role as a close and faithful companion was seen as a threat and used to drive a wedge between humans and the animal, in order to safeguard the supreme position that an almighty God was intended to play in the lives of men. What's more, as early Christianity grew, dogs, through a biblical influence, came to be associated with what were considered to be base human characteristics – prostitution, witchery and evil inclinations. The belief that God had accorded human beings absolute mastery over the animal world was thus used to condone the negative perception and treatment of dogs. [This relaxed during the thirteenth century] due to the influence of greater economic prosperity for the west, which loosened men's minds from narrow religious shackles and, as a result, assigned dogs a more benign reputation within the prevailing worldview. MARTINE

The Hebrews ... had migrated to the Nile region around 2500 BC. They reviled the dog, firstly, because of its dirty habits, and secondly, possibly because they were later enslaved by the Egyptians, who probably treated their dogs with more kindness and respect than they treated their slaves. Some notable biblical proverbs provide further clues including 'better a live dog than a dead lion' (Ecclesiastes 9:4) which meant there is always hope for the living – even a lowly dog – but none for the dead. JULIE

Jewish and Islamic scriptures treated [dogs] as particularly dirty animals and dogs were banned from many sacred sites in the Middle East and Greece. In the Bible, the word 'dog' is an insult or censure, or is used as a disparaging term for sinners. The Book of Revelation tells of the city of God, inside which are the blessed. Outside 'are the 'dogs', those who practise magic arts, the sexually immoral, the murderers, the idolaters and everyone who loves and practises falsehood'. Revelation asserts God's power over the souls of the dead and denies the power of pagan gods such as Hecate. Dog sacrifices will not guarantee entry to Heaven.

This passage may have been directly aimed at pagans who still worshipped Hecate, potentially the biggest rival to the Christian God in the first and second centuries. CHRIS

Dog days
Like Horace, like Johnson, like Churchill, like so many others, I will hold on, and wait for the dog days to end. CATE

The Romans used the term 'dog days' to describe the days when the Dog Star, Sirius, rises with the sun. These days were thought to be particularly unhealthy days. There was a belief that when the Dog Star rose over the rim of the sea the dogs would become angry and all the inhabitants of the land would be filled with fear and hatred. JOAN

The Dog Star [was] considered the doorway to the afterlife; its disappearance between July 3 and August 11 due to coincidence with the sun marked the so-called 'dog days' when the dead could not be buried. DEAN

In contrast to the view held by the ancient Greeks, Romans and Egyptians, many other peoples looked upon Sirius favourably, for instance Australian Aboriginals, early Hindu mythology, early Persians and many early astronomers. LUCY

Fate dogs Hecuba

The mythical figure of Queen Hecuba [wife of the Trojan king Priam and mother of Hector] cemented the association between depression and the black dog for the modern audience. One time queen of Troy, the story of her miserable fate has been passed down from the dawning days of Western literary culture. She appears in Homer's *Iliad*, and in two plays by Euripides. [In Ovid's version of the legend she was turned into a dog]:

> With Troy old Priam falls, his Queen survives;
> Till all her woes complete, transformed she grieves
> In borrowed Sounds, nor with a human face,
> Barking tremendous over the plains of Thrace.
> – Ovid, *Metamorphosis*[9] RAYMOND

Centuries later, Dante Alighieri in part one of *The Divine Comedy*, The Inferno (around 1300 AD), compared the insane gnashing and suffering of the Falsifiers in Hell with Hecuba's madness.

Hecuba darkens to Hecate

Hecuba changed over time into Hecate, who became demonised by Greek and Christian patriarchs alike and associated with ghosts, the hounds of hell, enchantment, sorcery and witchcraft, and the Empusae – vampiric goddesses. Medea was a priestess of Hecate.

Hecate is appeased by sacrifices of black lambs and dogs. She rules all crossroads. Suicides were often buried at crossroads, the practice continuing into Victorian times.

Hecate's pet, Cerberus

Sirius, [the] Dog Star, was the larger of Orion's two hunting-dogs. Hunting-dogs became associated with the ancient gods of Greek and Roman mythology, as did the guard dog of hell, Cerberus. Cerberus was a particularly blood-thirsty character. He lays down early mythic canine connections with death and sorrow. It is said he tormented the souls that entered hell, and devoured those who tried to escape. His three slavering heads (or more in some accounts), a lion's in the centre, and a dog's and wolf's on either side, were a formidable image to contemplate as an introduction to hell. His tail was serpent-like, with poisonous barbs. These are the two main roles, hunter and hell-hound, which lead to our current understanding of the Black Dog. SUE

[Hercules' Tenth Labour was to capture Cerebus]:

> The prudent Sibyl had before prepar'd
> A sop, in honey steep'd, to charm the guard;
> Which, mix'd with pow'rful drugs, she cast before
> His greedy grinning jaws, just op'd to roar.
> With three enormous mouths he gapes; and straight,
> With hunger press'd, devours the pleasing bait.
> – Virgil, *Aeneid VI* ANN

Ancient Greeks and bad humor

Primary exploration of the cause and manifestation of depression rests with the Greeks, who challenged the ancient belief that mental illness was the result of possession by supernatural forces. According to Hippocrates (460–377 BC), any type of mental disorder was instead very much due to natural causes – an imbalance in what had been defined by Empedocles, an earlier counterpart, as the four humors or main elements of the body (fire, earth, water, air). MARTINE

Hippocrates coined the word 'melancholia' from *melas-anos*, black, and *chole*, bile … Cicero (106–43 BC), a subsequent Roman philosopher, not only rejected Hippocrates' assumption, but proposed that emotional factors provoked physical malaise: 'What we call furor they call melancholia, as if the reason were affected by only a black bile [one of the four humors of the body], and not disturbed often by a violent rage, or fear, or grief' … As late as 1775, Samuel Johnson, himself a sufferer, in his great *Dictionary of the English Language* said melancholy was 'a disease arising from the Black Bile – or too heavy and viscous blood'. ALLAN

[Later in the second century, Galen (30?–90? AD), a Roman physician, insisted that] mental disease/disturbance of animal spirits [which were produced in the body from the transformation of food and air] arose either because the brain was directly afflicted (mania and melancholia) or because it was affected by disorder in another organ. ANN

[From the writings of Hippocrates]:

> Whoever wishes to investigate medicine properly, should proceed thus: in the first place to consider the seasons of the year ... For knowing the changes of the seasons, the risings and settings of the stars, how each of them takes a place, he will be able to know beforehand what sort of year is going to ensue ...
>
> One ought also to be guarded about the rising of the stars, especially of the Dogstar ... for diseases are especially apt to prove critical in those days ... But if the season is northerly and without water ... neither after the Dogstar nor Arcturus; this state agrees best with those who are naturally phlegmatic ... but it is most inimical to the bilious; for they become much parched up ... and in some cases melancholy.[10] LUCY

The dark disease of the mind, depression, was first recognised as a distinct illness as far back as the fifth and fourth centuries BC. The concept was introduced by Hippocrates ... it was defined by 'aversion to food, despondency, sleeplessness, irritability, restlessness,' as well as the statement that 'grief and fear, when lingering, provoke melancholia' ... Widely accepted until the Renaissance in the fourteenth century, the doctrine of the Four Humors stated that the balance of the four fluids of the human body, namely blood (*sanguis*), black bile (*melania chole*), yellow bile (*chole*), and phlegm (*phlegma*) determined the state of one's humors. The humors ... were defined as sanguine (optimistic), melancholic (depressive), choleric (short-tempered), and phlegmatic (unemotional). The humoral theory was further extended by Galen in the second century AD. Saturn was thought to promote accumulation of black bile which accumulation caused melancholy and madness. SARAH

The theory of humors continued on into the seventeenth century.

In the [Greek] medical books, melancholy was discussed as a disease, which could be treated in certain ways, including listening to music, flogging or cauterisation. WIZY

The most avant-garde [doctor] of his time, Asclepiades, rejected the then common practices carried out in the interest of mental health: bloodletting, mechanical restraint and incarceration in cells ... and advocated the humanistic treatment of the mentally ill in pleasant surroundings. The Romans, like the Greeks, saw a physical origin to diseases of the mind, according to Theodore Millon.[11] Asclepiades was the first person to argue that biologically and chemically based treatments could be exceptionally beneficial ... TERESA

Less humane treatment

A plague was raging in the city of Ephesus, and they asked Apollonius to be the physician at their infirmary.

When he arrived at Ephesus he assembled the population at the theatre, and told them to stone to death an old blind beggar who stood there. The people were at first reluctant to do so, but they eventually approached the task with sufficient energy as to completely bury the old man under a pile of thrown stones. When the stones were removed, the old man had been transformed into a giant black dog; proof that all along he had been an evil spirit and responsible for the plague. PETER

Dogs of Rome

[While the dog] once carried rabies and other diseases into our villages and towns ... yet it should be remembered that it also suckled the founders of Rome and was our only guide and protector, in many old myths. BARBARA

Pliny (23–79 AD), a Roman naturalist, encyclopaedist and writer [wrote] of the healing properties of dogs. Overwhelmingly though, during Greco-Roman times, dogs were used as sacrifices. Plutarch (c.46–120 AD), the Greek biographer, recorded that black puppies were often sacrificed to appease the gods (especially at the rising of the Dog Star). CAROL

The Romans were more inclined to follow the Greek belief that dogs are faithful, but dirty and shameless ... The Romans believed that the Dog Star, Sirius, added to the heat of the summer months when the star was in its ascendancy ... [and] that dogs were frequently driven crazy by the excess heat. The dog [began] to symbolise inferiority, spuriousness or some other mongrel quality, as in the metaphors 'dog Latin', meaning an inferior, or corrupt, form of the classical Latin language, and 'dog's logic', meaning that little or no care was used in developing an argument. JULIE

During the Roman period [the] cult [of Anubis] was singled out for abuse by Roman writers. This may have been partly because of his popularity with necromancers [who practised divination by raising the spirits of the dead; there is a subsidiary meaning in the form 'nigromancy', in which the magical force of 'dark powers' is gained from or by acting upon corpses]. Anubis was used as the go-between to fetch gods and spirits from the Underworld to answer the magician's questions ... and as an enforcer of curses ... Thus Anubis was transformed into a feared and hated being who sought the souls of innocent and guilty alike, and who represented eternal torture. MARCELLA

Because of the relationship between dogs and the afterlife, they were assumed to be able to tell when death was approaching. In classical literature, the howling of dogs is frequently an omen of some tragedy. Dogs were said to have bayed through Rome prior to the split between Julius Caesar and the general Pompey that led to civil war. Dogs later howled before Caesar's murder and before the death of Emperor Maximinus, among others. CHRIS

[Belief in the werewolf] had its origins with the Roman poet Ovid, who told the story of Lycaon, who changed into a wolf, howled, became savage –'his own savage nature showed in his rabid jaws' ...

This belief became much stronger in the Middle Ages. JOAN

MULTICULTURAL
BLACK DOGS

There are strikingly similar cross-cultural traditions about the passage to the Otherworld …

The Hindu god of death, Yama … employs two black dogs to bring back wandering souls. HARRIET

Historically, since man first domesticated the dog (from before 11 000 BC, probably initially from around Mesopotamia), the animal was documented as being linked to Zoroastrian funeral rites … Zoroastrians were concerned for the well-being of dogs, and this was thought to avert the Evil Eye and to accrue merit … Humans have associated dogs with death, war and scavenging since these early times. VIVIENNE

The Andean culture has it that there is a river guarded by black dogs. If people have been 'good' they are ferried to the other side. But the wicked are refused and their souls have to roam forever. The idea of a symbolic river to cross is echoed in the Christian tradition of St Christopher who was supposed to have carried the Christ Child over a river, and became the patron saint of travellers. Much older than this legend, however, comes the idea that St Christopher was dog headed, and one of the race of *cynocephali*. This seems to have originated amongst the ancient religions of the East, recalling one of the gods of Egypt called Atrum who was dog-headed and associated with devouring the souls of the dead. It may have originated out of Africa with, perhaps, skins of dog-headed baboons being brought from the region and examined, thus giving credence to the idea of a dog-headed race. LOIS

In the Parsee religion the dog is also the guardian of the underworld. He guarded the bridge where souls were judged. In the Aztec tradition, Xoltl, the god of death and the setting sun, had a dog's head. In China the dog at night symbolised destruction and catastrophe. The Chinese also depicted chaos in the shape of a huge shaggy dog ... The Hindus brought the idea of demon and dog together in the name *rakshas*, which means 'demon-dogs'. The leader of the pack, Ravana, had ten heads and twenty arms, copper-coloured eyes and 'a crescent of teeth like the young moon'. He represented the forces of evil. JOAN

In Chinese mythology, the T'ien kon hsing or 'Heavenly Dog Star' is an unlucky star which 'devours the moon' at the time of an eclipse and thus blacks it out ... and dogs are frequently associated with Buddhist immortals ... Carvings ... depict Izenshun [a Buddhist sage] riding on the back of a black dog. The legend relates that at one time in his travels Izenshun met up with a strange black dog, which animal's attentions he could not shake off. This black dog literally dogged the sage's footsteps all the way home and thereafter clung closely to him. From that time on, the unwilling host was forced to feed and care for the uninvited beast. One day the supernatural black dog transformed itself into a black dragon, which then took Sennin Izenshun up to heaven on its back. KEITH

Guardian dogs occur widely in shamanic Otherworldly lore. A dog with bared teeth guards the entrance to the undersea land of the Mother of the Sea Beasts, in

Eskimo shamanism. Similar depictions occur in African and Indian mythology. MARY

In Afghan folklore, a dog guards the underworld realm of Erlik Khan, the lord of chaos ... In Catalan myth, Dip is an evil, black, hairy dog, a messenger of the Devil, and he sucks people's blood. ALLAN

Japanese people were accustomed to shooting dead a black dog in a religious ceremony. But this was during a rainmaking ceremony and black dogs were chosen because their hair imitated the colour of rain clouds. JEFFREY

In central Australia, Kurpany, a huge black dog, attacks the Mala people who are having an Inma (ceremony); the dog kills many of the tribe's people, chasing the rest south. The Inma which has been disrupted is a religious ceremony of sorts that brings happiness and security to a tribe by way of a ritualistic coming together. RUPERT

In the horse sacrifice of ancient India (in writings dated around 800 BC but referring to Vedic traditions already established), a dog that has black colouration around its eyes, 'suggesting the guardian dogs of the land of the dead', was a symbol of misfortune. [As shown in the National Museum of Anthropology] in Mexico, from pre-classical times (from 1000 BC), the dog was intimately connected with death, since it was customary to bury dead people with sacrificed dogs or with ceramic figures of dogs; possibly the idea was that the dog should guide the soul of the deceased on its journey to the underworld. The Menomini Indians of North America believe in a journey of death, in the course of which a wide river is encountered; across it is a bridge, guarded by a great dog. In India, Bhairava (an aspect of Siva the Destroyer) is usually accompanied by two black dogs; dogs (particularly black ones) were often considered the most appropriate sacrifice to him. In Sri Lanka, the demon Mahasona uses a black dog or boar as its vehicle. ANN

The cry uttered at [Irish] funerals was known as the caoin or keen, derived from the Greek *kuvos* (a dog). ROBERT

Dogs as companions

Ancient Celtic funeral traditions buried a person's dog with them as companions and protectors in the afterlife. GREG

[In the] ancient Chinese ritual of burial … the Western Chou and the An-Yang, 770 BC, buried their dead in wooden coffins set in the bottom of a pit-grave over a small pit for the 'soul-conducting' dog … a demonstration of the psychopomp performing his duty to guide the departed soul on the path to the Otherworld.

In ancient times 'when a new graveyard was opened, the first person to be buried there was charged with the responsibility of guarding all who came after'; later this was thought to be too onerous a duty, so 'a large black dog was installed for the purpose'.[12] HEATHER

There is a legend of this sort about a church in Picton, New South Wales (see pages 112–13):

It was customary to sacrifice a dog, specifically one without one white hair, in the foundations of the church.[13]

The ascendancy of the church in Europe
Now a gap in the literature emerges ...

... that stretches from the birth of Dante in 1265 back to the death of Horace in 8 BC, and can be divided into two periods.

The first is the Dark [or early Middle] Ages (500–1100 AD) in which pagan learning and classics gradually disappeared [or were adapted] as Christianity took hold. Other factors that compounded the situation were the decline of towns as the people turned to agricultural and pastoral pursuits, and the change from the Roman emperors (central government) to semi-barbaric Teutonic kings (feudal system of government).

The second is in the decline in classical thought and culture in ancient Greece and Rome ... which started around the death of Horace and became progressively worse after the end of 200 AD. LUCY

YE OLDE
BLACKE DOGGE

And darkness fills the space
As myth and man embrace.
FRED CURTIS

The mythical world remained so integral a part of Celtic society that when Christianity arrived, the spoken myths could not be destroyed. Instead they were often Christianised or given Christian endings. JEAN

Why the Dark Ages?

The Dark Ages – the period of the early Middle Ages between Rome's decline (400 AD) and around 1100 AD – saw an inrush of Germanic invaders on land, brigands at sea and Arab conquests in the east at the cessation of the *pax romana* (the 'Roman peace', the relative order that prevailed when the armies of ancient Rome policed the western world). The Christian church preserved some local stability, but it was a time of ignorance, fear and poverty. Europe began to revive by 1100 AD, with centres of learning (future universities) growing around the cathedrals.

Before the introduction of the printing press in the fifteenth century, books were written laboriously by hand (*manu* and *scripti* are the Latin words for 'by hand' and 'written'). Many of the more important manuscripts were decorated with portraits and heraldic emblems beautifully picked out with gold leaf and coloured pigments and known as illuminated scripts.

Since writing skills were mainly found in the monasteries, the church was the major influence on the tenor of the knowledge that was disseminated.

Biblical black dogs

The symbolism of black dogs was twofold: faithful servant and terrible omen [an omen is a phenomenon that is supposed to portend good or evil; a prophetic sign of something about to happen]. The Bible, though, does not make any reference to the positive qualities of dogs, associating them almost exclusively with heresy and sin. People continued to keep companion dogs and working dogs, but it was this biblical treatment of dogs that shaped European superstition and belief through the Middle Ages. CHRIS

The most important corollary to the medieval development of the metaphor [black dog] ... is that it had
gained more sinister connotations. Not only was the
black dog a sentry at the gates to the afterlife, but in its
new role, the black dog was making unwanted advances
in the realm of the living. DANIEL

And the Devil take the hindermost

The treatment of individuals thought to suffer from
depression has ranged from the tempered thinking of
ancient Greece to the intractable moralising of the
Middle Ages wherein perceived indications of depressive diseases were generally considered symptomatic of
the Devil and seized as damning evidence of individual
sinfulness. FRANCES

[In the] seventh century [there was an] onslaught of
religious dogma that served to identify the Devil as 'a
culprit for all types of deviant behaviour and
Demonology [as] the "psychiatry" of the day.'[14] This
renewed belief in the link between supernatural forces
and mental illness persisted into the fifteenth century,
with sufferers not branded as victims, but sinners.
MARTINE

Jeffrey Burton Russell (*Lucifer, the Devil in the Middle
Ages*)[15] ... notes that during the Middle Ages
demonology became distinctly Christianised ... many
anathema pagan animal gods, along with those of the
earlier Judaeo-Christian traditions, became identified
as those whose shape the Devil would choose to
assume ... an adder, bee, camel, dog, goat, fish, gnat,
lion, pig, rooster, whale, worm, in fact an entire

menagerie of creatures, the most frequent of which were serpent, goat and dog.

The ubiquitous stray dog, encountered on a dark night, shaggy, growling and barely visible but for its frightening eyes, was surely destined to become embedded across European folklore as a fearsome spectre, in a way less [available] to the occasional recalcitrant snake, goat, pig or fish. Russell also states that 'the theological distinction between the Devil as Prince of Evil and his followers the demons is often blurred in folklore'. We have, therefore, a situation in which it was commonly believed that a stray dog could be a demon in disguise. BARBARA

The Devil's door was placed on the north side of some old churches to let the Devil out at baptism, as north was perceived to be the Devil's side where Satan and his legions lurked, to catch the unwary. MARY

The noonday demon

Christine Read, in her book *Depression: Lifting the Cloud*,[16] alludes to a passage from the Book of Job in the Old Testament:

> Yet when I hoped for good, evil came;
> When I looked for light, then came darkness.
> The churning inside me never stops;
> Days of suffering confront me.
> I go about blackened, but not by the sun …
> ALLAN

Whether the Book of Job was referring specifically to depression, or to spiritual suffering arising from loss of faith, is debatable. But certainly internal suffering was spoken about in terms of blackness. By the Middle Ages the Christian Church was calling depression *accidie*, but the darkness remained closely associated with despair, the absence of hope, the loss of God's light.

Accidie was described, by Dante among others, as the sin of sloth – in its extreme form, the sin of despair. Also known as the 'noonday demon', it was the sense of futility that undermined faith in God, and encompassed the failure to do what was spiritually beneficial. The counter to sloth was action.

Writers as diverse in their religious opinions as Burton and Sibbes agreed that melancholy was 'Satan's bath'. The Devil exploited the weakened reason and over-powerful imaginations of people sickened by melancholy and tempted them to despair of their salvation.[17]

Dogs of the Lord

The Crusades (from the eleventh to the thirteenth centuries) were mounted by the church to win back the Holy Land from Islam. Islam eventually triumphed, but invited the Christians back as pilgrims to share the best of Greco–Roman culture. From this sprang a new world of scientific knowledge and material wealth. This was a challenge to the foundations of medieval Christendom, and the church reacted by defining deviation from set belief as heresy. Crusades were then sent to combat heretics, and a savage ecclesiastical court, the Inquisition, was instituted (and continued for several hundred years), run by the Dominicans or Black Friars, the Dogs of the Lord (*domini canes*).

Black death

The Black Death ('black' because of subdermal haemorrhage, and perhaps related more to an Ebola-like virus than to the bubonic plague) appeared first in 1334 in north-eastern China. 'The Great Pestilence', as it came to be called, reached Europe in 1348 and struck the crowded cities of Europe, killing 25 million people – over four years nearly half the population of Europe was wiped out. The bubonic plague continued to strike Europe, with decreasing fatality, every ten to twenty years in short-lived outbreaks right up to the 1700s.

Religious fervour and fanaticism peaked, with savage persecution of minorities such as Jews, lepers (skin disorders were seen as an outward sign of a defective soul), the mentally ill, those deemed to be witches, and individuals who were unconventional in any way. The spectre of the Black Death dominated art and literature: the imagery of *la danse macabre* is from this time; an allegory on the universality of death, regardless of one's station in life.

Bubble, bubble, toil and trouble

As Christianity grew in popularity, so did theories of demonology, and sufferers of all forms of mental disturbance were treated with the frenzied cruelty and contempt of the righteous. During the witch hunts between the thirteenth and sixteenth centuries, many sufferers of mental illness were incarcerated or burnt at the stake to safeguard good honest people from those 'possessed' by delusions and hallucinations. Depression, nestling in a quieter spot than the more manifest behavioural antics of the mentally deranged, was commonly unnoticed and undiagnosed. If sufferers were lucky enough to escape the dungeon or stake, they quietly sank deeper into their lonely desperation … JOANNE

Hecate, the Roman goddess of the crossroads, was frequently depicted with the head of a dog:

[Hecate re-emerged in the Middle Ages as] the Queen of the Witches. This new role for Hecate was most famously exploited by Shakespeare in Macbeth: hers is the spectre summoned by the three witches in the cavern scene. DANIEL

In 1603 King James published *Daemonologie*, the doctrine of witchcraft, in which he set out that not all witches are melancholics influenced by the Devil, but that some individuals invoke infernal aid to assist in their lust for riches or revenge.

Looks like a witch

A damning description [from the time] that stereotyped witches:

> Women which be commonly old, lame, bleareyed, pale, and full of wrinkles; poor, sunken, superstitious and papists ... They are lean and deformed, showing melancholy in their faces, to the horror of all that sees them.[18] LUCY

To the simple godfearing folk of the time, a [woman] acting strangely was deemed to be evil, a witch. The witch figure possessed medicinal properties and the ability to offer mixtures of various plants for treatment of ailments. These were independent, free-thinking and self-empowered people ... Later they were linked with Satan. Banned from the villages, they were ostracised and feared by their fellows, and blamed for every disaster that overtook the village. Extreme physical and psychological torture was used to extract 'confessions' from those accused and, worse, many confessed to crimes they didn't do. VIVIENNE

The witch's familiar

Feminist scholarship suggests additional perspectives on dogs. Arguing from the widespread appearance of

THE DEVIL INTRODUCES A
WITCH TO HER FAMILIAR[19]

dogs as 'companions of the Goddess in many cultures, long before gods or men appeared with canine companions', [Barbara] Walker concludes that women were the first to domesticate the dog. She argues that the dog 'tended to be diabolised along with the Goddess's other traditional companions', with the decline of goddess worship in the Middle East, giving rise to insulting use not only of the term 'son of a bitch' but also 'dog'. Later, black dogs were associated with witches. 'The dog was frequently believed to be the animal form of a demon lover, probably because women were inclined to fondle their dogs; many women were hanged in England on that count alone.' As the witch's helper in gathering materials for charms, dogs came to be associated with curses. This may underlie the slang use of 'dog' for an unpleasant woman.[20] ROBIN

Invariably the accused alleged, in his/her defence, accounts of a 'familiar', frequently a black dog, as having been the creature who compelled him/her to commit the act of black magic. HEATHER

Not only black cats but black dogs were associated with unfortunate old women (marked as witches), and these animals were suspected of being witches' familiars, taking the animal form of a demon lover. The dogs were also supposed to help the witch in preparing her charms by digging up the mandrake root sometimes known as 'the Devil's genitals'. This was supposed to give forth a scream if uprooted by others, who might then go mad or die. LOIS

The *Malleus Maleficarum* (*The Witches' Hammer*) was published in 1486, and was used by Inquisitors as a guide to the identification, prosecution, and dispatch of witches. Though many Christian scholars and theologians doubted the existence of witches and largely regarded such belief as superstition, the authors of the *Malleus* declared that 'the Belief that there are such Beings as Witches is so Essential a Part of the Catholic Faith that Obstinacy to maintain the Opposite Opinion manifestly savours of Heresy'. The popular adoption of the *Malleus* meant that any who questioned it were at risk of being branded heretics.[21]

Ergot you, babe

Rye is the main crop in the colder lands of northern and western Europe, where most reports of Black Dogs of all kinds have come from since Roman times. Rye is the most notorious host for *claviceps purpurea*, the ergot fungus. In moist seasons especially, this fungus infests a huge percentage of the ripening grain heads, poisoning the whole of the crop with ergotamine ... from which the hallucinogen lysergic acid [LSD] is derived – along with many other highly toxic agents, the sum of which can have serious and sometimes deadly effects ... The evil presence of *roggenwulf*, 'rye wolf', has been greatly feared, and the last sheaf of rye, known as the 'wolf's tooth', is tied up securely in order to imprison the wolf himself. He is almost certainly the basis for the lycanthropic tales which have so long persisted, and which at times are boosted by outbreaks of the fungus.

Ergotism causes everything needed to explain everything reported about Black Dogs of all kinds. Paranoid delusions. Hallucinations. Spasms. Necrosis. Bizarre behaviour. Quasi-religious experiences. Depression. And, of course, Death, both by direct effects of the toxins, and by suicide. BRUCE

St Anthony's Fire was the name of a disorder that was probably caused by ergot poisoning. And perhaps Black Shuck (shuck meaning a husk of corn nowadays) owes something to the anxiety occasioned by the discovery of ergot infection in the current crop.

There is evidence that the Salem witch trials in America (1692) followed an outbreak of rye ergot. And a study of demographics, weather, literature and crop records from Europe and America found that drops in population have followed diets heavy in rye bread and weather that favours ergot. During the huge depopulation in the early years of the Black Death, after 1347, conditions were ideal for ergot. This may well have contributed to the hysteria of the later witch hunts.[22]

The beginnings of psychiatry

The witchcraft ruse was eventually put to sleep, thanks to the efforts of early psychiatry. A Flemish physician, Jan de Weir (1515–1588), who is credited with founding psychiatry, published a book in 1563 called *De Praestigiis Daemonum* (*About the Activities of Devils*). The following extract outlines de Wier's views on the unscientific nature of judging mental illnesses as 'witchcraft':

> The uninformed and unskilled physicians relegate all the incurable diseases, or the diseases the remedy for which they overlook to witchcraft … In all such cases a good doctor is to be consulted because nothing is more important than to make the clinical situations as clear as daylight, for in no domain of human life are human passions so freely at play as in this one, these passions being superstition, rage, hate and malice.[23] JULIE

Medieval maladies and mixtures

Treatment choices for any illness consisted of spells, folk medicine and herbal remedies, mysticism, prayer and astrology. Destiny, sin and astral influences determined the course and outcome of disease and injury. One might have had one's forehead burnt to release the demons, or had religious delusions interpreted as a sign of sainthood. Pagan cures, incantations and spells were popular, though forbidden by the church; thus many archaic spells were given a Christian flavour invoking God and the saints. Practitioners included university-trained physicians, monks and folk healers, depending on the patient's class. Each type of healer was distrustful of the others.

Europe in both the Middle Ages and the Renaissance

suffered massive epidemics, diseases of overcrowded and unsanitary cities; but the concept of infection was unclear, and it was thought that disease was due to the influence of the stars, or something that developed in the body due to catching something from the atmosphere; or that, in contagion, the humours could become a form of species. Thus the unbalanced humour was balanced out or purged with herbal remedies, bloodletting or laxatives; plague victims, understood to be contagious, were quarantined and isolated and lepers were exiled; but syphilis became virulent and was treated with mercury, bismuth and arsenic compounds.

Arsenic was still used in the treatment of syphilis in the early days at Prince Henry, the isolation hospital at Little Bay, Sydney.

Star struck and in a bad humor

On the humor of melancholy lies the reason why so many a sleeper cries for fear of a black bull or a black bear or that black devils have him by the hair:

> Certes, this dreem which ye han met tonight
> Cometh of greet superfluytee
> Of youre rede colera, pardee,
> Which causeth folk to dreden in hir dremes
> Of arwes, and of fyre with rede lemes,
> Of grete beestes, that they wol hem byte,
> Of contek, and of whelpes grete and lyte;
> Right as the humor of malencholie
> Causeth ful many a man in sleep to crie
> For feere of blake beres, or boles blake,
> Or elles blake develes wole him take.
> – Chaucer (c.1340–1400), The Nun's Priest's Tale,
> *The Canterbury Tales* LUCY

In these Dog Days it is forbidden by Astronomy to all Manner of People to be let blood or to take Physic. Yea, it is good to abstain all this time from Women. For why, all that time reigneth a Star that is called Canicula Canis, a Hound in English, and the kind of the Star is burning or broiling as fire. All this time the Heat of the Sun is so fervent and violent that Men's bodies at Midnight sweat as at Midday; and if they be hurt, they may be more sick than at any other time, yea, very near dead ... – *The Husbandman's Practice*, 1729 LOIS

Hospitals, pilgrimage and folk healers

Most formal medicine was practised by the church, which saw illness as divine retribution. The sick took pilgrimages in the hope of recovering by making peace with God. Monks applied learning from ancient medical texts, using herbal remedies from plants cultivated in their gardens. The earliest hospitals were established by monasteries, and were primarily refuges for the old and disabled and for travelling pilgrims.

Medicine for the general populace, usually performed by women, relied on folk and herbal remedies passed down by elders. Later religious persecution and witch-hunting led to the execution of thousands of folk healers who were so skilled that they were thought to have a pact with the Devil.[24]

The monk's, the witch's and the alchemist's garden

Mandrake was a must in the garden. Associated with fertility, sleep, war (Mars), prosperity and an ability to foretell the future, it was a good all-rounder. It was used as an anaesthetic, and also had purgative, emetic and demon-expelling qualities. It was known as 'the Devil's Candle', or lewder names. However, harvesting it was a problem ...

Mandrakes were plants first introduced into Britain in the eleventh century. It is well documented that black dogs, tempted by a nearby piece of meat, were the creatures deemed suitable to remove a mandrake plant from the ground by pulling it up with a rope around their necks. This was because of their black colour, which represented evil and death.

The mandrake plant was said to shriek in such a ghastly manner when extracted that all who heard the sound would die instantly – including the dog (until dogs apparently grew immune and were ritually slaughtered instead). This shriek has been interpreted culturally as the ultimate expression of spiritual horror and despair. The dog sometimes died from strangulation by the rope, which no doubt prompted depression in his immediate family and forerunners of the RSPCA.

The whole point of digging up a mandrake (*Mandragora*) was to access its properties, which were those of belladonna. These were used for sedatives, anaesthetics or aphrodisiacs. The dead dog was, in a sense, a hero or saviour, who gave his life to establish a nascent pharmaceutical industry. The palliatives cooked up from the mandrakes were the closest things they had to antidepressants in former centuries ... Greek physician Discorides (c.60 AD) noted that mandrake juice 'doth expel upward Phlegm and black choler'. JEFFREY

Science's precursor: Alchemy

Alchemy, a forerunner of modern chemistry, was rooted in Arab and Greek culture. Its main goal was to transmute base metals into gold and bring wealth to all (or maybe just to the alchemist). This transmutation required a substance, as yet undiscovered, known as the philosopher's stone, which was also allied with the elixir of life, or *panacea*, a remedy for all diseases, evils and difficulties, able to promote spiritual reawakening.

Alchemy employed the four elements: fire, representing the emotions of anger and grief with the heart as its organ; air, representing the emotion of attachment, and the lungs; water, linked with desire, and the kidney; and earth, allied with fear, and the liver.

Alchemists ascribed disease to 'infectious seeds' rather than to imbalance of the four humors, rejected blood-letting and believed that like cures were required for like ailments. Alchemy was restricted to men: in the hands of a woman it was witchcraft. Medicinal alchemy was still in use during the Renaissance.

> There is an extraordinary storehouse of images and ideas that profoundly influenced European philosophy, literature and art during the sixteenth century. Alongside Christianity, the alchemical or hermetic tradition persisted in Europe, despite times of falling into disrepute. Notwithstanding the claims of transmuting base metals into gold, the secret art of alchemy lay in personal transformation. [Alchemists] worked with the symbolic process of transformation which they understood to begin in chaos (blackness and depression) and to end with the birth of the new unified personality.
>
> One of the stages of alchemical work involved a terrible depression and blackness that the alchemists called '*nigredo*' or melancholia, 'a black blacker than black', an affliction of the soul. In one treatise this was represented as a wounding caused by a 'rabid black dog'. There are frequent references to the dog in alchemical texts, drawing on both the 'light' and 'dark' symbolism. In its dark aspect, the dog represented the dark side of the moon, and the dangers of the destructive stages of the chemical opus. HOLLY

Black in alchemical context is said to represent the 'absence of colour; the first stage of the Great Work'.[25] [In alchemy, black is typified by base lead.] The symbolism of this might suggest that depression offers the opportunity for transmutation, rebirth, but that it constitutes only the first stage in the development *opus* of the individual, the transformation of the inner or psychic 'lead' into 'gold'. JENNIFER

Faith in alchemy fell away after the Black Death devastated Europe. It was the norm for treatment, and used by most scientists and doctors before and during the Black Death, but its potions and 'cures' proved ineffective. One legacy that remained was *liquor* (distilled alcohol), commonly applied as a remedy, and as a result its consumption rose dramatically.

CRY WOLF!

Traces of fear and respect for wolves – which can grow up to two metres long, weigh up to 80 kilograms, and once lived throughout Europe, the Americas and Asia – are … retained in our language in phrases like 'cry wolf', 'keep the wolf from the door', 'throw someone to the wolves', 'a wolf in sheep's clothing'. FRED

Beowulf is a tale from Sweden that was written down around 1000 AD. The tale was, however, known long before this, having been played by minstrels for centuries. It is acknowledged as the earliest epic poem written in English, and dates to the seventh or eighth century AD in the time of Anglo-Saxon rule. The dog features in an evil role as Beowulf's adversary Grendel, and he and his mother are depicted as lupine. ROSLYN

[Superstitions about] ... changelings, werewolves/ lycanthropes, Black Shuck, [perhaps came from] the old Norse invaders and their gods, led by one-eyed All-father Odin (Woden), master of magic and discoverer of the Runes, and his ghostly hounds of war. [On stormy nights Odin, riding his eight-legged horse through the air, led the Wild Hunt, accompanied by monstrous greedy black dogs thought to be demons. The Hunt would collect the souls of the dying or newly dead and drive them to Hell.]

The savage warriors that worshipped these northern gods were the murderous thugs and rapists known as beserkers, who wore the skins of wolves or bears in battle and must have resembled changelings or huge and diabolical, wolf-like creatures that were possessed by a terrible, possibly alcohol-induced, insane battle fury. FRED

Where, oh where has my little dog gone?

A werewolf was a human who changed into a wolf, due to magic or a curse. The transformation sometimes happened with the rising of the full moon. It was a form of shape-shifting, the phenomenon of changing from human to animal form (often a wolf) or vice versa, or from one person into another. One way in which the idea may have arisen is from the Norse berserkers, dressed in their animal skins.

Werewolves were believed to have originally been disturbed humans. They were transformed into big, ferocious black dogs or wolves ... JOAN

Werewolves … were almost universal in the mythology of all countries to which dogs were native. VIVIENNE

Burton wrote *The Anatomy of Melancholy* in 1621, and in this study of melancholy he connects … werewolves with 'black choler' (bile), even saying that the werewolf was a manifestation of the Devil. JOAN

Lycanthropia [was] called by some *'melancholia canina'* … The condition was described by fourth century writer, Marcellus:

> you will recognise those who are so affected by these signs: they are pale; their vision is weak, they have dry eyes, and they don't shed tears. They also have dog bites … But you should know that this is a species of melancholy.[26] SUZANNE

Symptoms of the disease … porphyria (genetic metabolic disorder – depiction of the condition in the film *The Madness of King George III*) can include red pigmentation of the eyes and gums, a distortion of the upper lip into a snarl, hypertrichosis (abnormal growth of hair) on the forehead, arms and legs, distorted limbs, curling nails, and an aversion to light that condemns the sufferer to go out only at night. Given the tradition of shape-shifting in many cultures, this encouraged a belief in werewolves. Since another symptom of porphyria can be manic depression, this is yet another link between 'possession by a dog' and depression. ANN

Demon dogs

Take care, an imp is upon your heel.
You feel his fetid touch as he passes by
Or sense him padding up close behind

Whilst on the back of your neck his breath
Is stale, forewarning of incubi.
He's black, he's lean, a fiend with the evil eye
And blooded jaw, it is said, he's part
Of monk and part of hound and the Devil's spore,
An awful creature whose spectral cry
Is heard above the shriek of the highest gale;
He stalks alone when the twilight fades,
Don't catch his eye or else you will die –
He's Shuck, the Demon Dog and the marshland's bale.
FRED CURTIS

God knows with what effect on local postmen! JEFFREY

There were legends of the black dog which was said to roam the English countryside from as far back as Viking times.

One name for him was 'Black Shuck', which came from an Anglo-Saxon word *scucca* [or *succa*] meaning 'demon'. He was a 'large black hellhound, the size of a calf, with flaming eyes'. In the north of England he was known as Barghest [from the German *'bargeist'*, spirit of the funeral bier], in Wales he was 'Gwyllgi', 'a frightful apparition of a mastiff with baleful breath and blazing red eyes'. In Wales and on the Norfolk coast the black dog was supposed to be amphibious, coming out of the sea by night and travelling about the lonely lanes. In Jersey he was 'Tchico', and on the Isle of Man, 'Mauthe Doog'. He was seen mainly at night and was an omen of death. Black Shuck is sometimes headless ... JOAN

Usually the phantom dog is black ... It is always large, bigger than the biggest dog ... calf-size. The coat is often shaggy, and the other main feature described is the creature's eyes, said to be glowing or even red or fiery. Their habit has been to appear out of thin air, scare the hell out of people, and bring death to them within a calendar year (the extra day in Leap Year, I suppose, being tossed in as a bonus, or bone). JEFFREY

There is a contemporary account from Abraham Fleming, recounted by many of our essayists. In a diary entry dated 9 am, Sunday 4 August, 1577, he describes the apparition of a demon dog which tore through St Mary's Church in Bungay, England, during a terrific storm. It appeared

> in a most horrible similitude and likenesse to the congregation then and there present, a dog as they might discerne it, of a black colour; at the site whereof, togither with the fearful flashes of fire which were then seene, moved such admiration in the minds of the assemblie, that they thought doomesday was already come ... this black dog, or the divil in such a likenesse (God hee knoweth all who worketh all) running all along down the body of the church with great swiftnesse and incredible haste.[27]

It wrung the necks of two people, shrivelled another and then proceeded to the church in Blythburgh and slew a couple more.

> Black dogs were seen as inhabiting border areas between different realms of existence. This dovetails with the fact that British hellhounds were frequently spotted at crossing points like stiles, bridges and gates [Hecate's territory]. They were also believed to walk along *ley lines* – supposedly straight lines connecting ancient sites of spiritual significance. It seems to me more likely that they patrolled straight lines between chunks of food, but superstition gave them less meal-oriented motives. JEFFREY

Black dogs 🐕
Dogs of other colours 🐕

MAIN AREAS OF BLACK DOG SIGHTINGS IN THE UK[28]
FORTEAN PICTURE LIBRARY, HENBLAS, MWROG STREET, RUTHIN, LL15 1LG, UK.
HTTP://WWW.FORTEANPIX.DEMON.CO.UK/

Recorded mythology ... shows most sightings have been attributed to roadways, usually at night. Other places [include] old footpaths, track-ways, bridges, crossroads, gates, doors, stairs, corridors and gallows sites (probably because the gallows were on a crossroad). Another common place are graves and barrows. The dogs also haunted the ley lines of the earth (possibly because of the magnetic forces attributed to ley lines) and features known as corpse ways or spirit paths. Ancient paths such as these, so folklore tells us, used to run between churches with graveyards, and it was believed spirits travelled from graveyard to graveyard. J0

Ley lines (or dragon-lines), a term coined by Alfred Watkinson in 1921, refers to the earth's network of electromagnetic flows. The term 'ley' is derived from an old Anglo-Saxon word meaning 'a forest clearing'. Watkinson's theory was that ancient sites – mounds, moats, beacon hills and fords – around Britain lay on 'trackways' that were in alignment with each other, linked by tracks used by prehistoric traders in salt, flint and (later) metals. Churches had then been built on such pagan sites to 'Christianise' them. Some people believe that the castles on these sites are haunted by *glaistigs*, or fairy women.

And a dreadful thing from the cliff did spring,
And its wild bark thrill'd around,
His eyes had the glow of the fires below,
'Twas the form of the spectre hound.
– Old Norfolk poem

Such stories functioned as cautionary tales. Don't break away from the group. The stories of dangerous and otherworldly black dogs warned listeners, especially children, of the perils of taking the path less travelled, both literally and figuratively, of moving away from the warmth and familiarity of social contact.

The dog further afield

Stories of the ghost Black Dog known as the Grim span the Atlantic, stretching from graveyards in the UK to cemeteries in the USA, particularly in slave burial grounds. [Leanne] Dempsey asserts that visitors who linger in these graveyards after sunset are chased off by the resident angry black ghost dog. These hounds are thought to be spiritual guardians protecting the dead from the living, an interesting twist to an old ghost story theme. GILLIAN

In the town of Meridan, Connecticut, there is a folk saying that 'If a man shall meet the black dog once, it shall be for joy; and if twice, it shall be for sorrow; and if the third time, he shall die'. DANIEL

Dogs get better press

How many famous faithful hounds there are in history! Argos, Odysseus's dog in Homer's *Odyssey*, recognises his master on his return after twenty years' absence, and is so pleased to see him that he dies of joy. From the Middle Ages my more diminutive relatives are placed at the foot of ladies' tombs to denote faithfulness and affection, and placed at the foot of crusaders' tombs to represent their faithful following of the armies of the Lord. These dogs are examples of beneficent companions, and I am a far more malevolent force. Yet I too am the unerring companion that these other dogs so often represent. HARRIET

From the Middle Ages onwards dogs were represented more positively. The dog in medieval Christian art usually symbolised faithfulness. In later Western art dogs became associated with the aristocracy; noblemen were often painted with their favourite dogs ... In legend and literature, the positive side of canine nature was associated with 'hound' rather than 'dog'. The faithfulness and persistence of hounds was celebrated in poetry and song, as in *John Peel*, 'with his hounds and his horn in the morning', and [Francis Thompson's] mystical poem *The Hound of Heaven*:

> I fled Him, down the nights and down the days;
> I fled Him, down the arches of the years;
> I fled Him, down the labyrinthine ways
> Of my own mind; and in the mist of tears
> I hid from Him, and under running laughter.
> Up vistaed hopes I sped;
> And shot, precipitated,
> Adown Titanic glooms of chasmèd fears,
> From those strong Feet that followed, followed after.
> But with unhurrying chase,
> And unperturbèd pace ...
>
> KAREN

In medieval England, packs of hunting dogs were a common sight in the large country homes. Dogs that didn't behave were hung. Dog-fights had also become a common spectator sport. From this we get metaphors such as 'dog-eat-dog', which meant to be utterly ruthless, and 'dogs of war', which pertained to the fierceness with which dogs would fight each other. JULIE

What a knight it was

During the twelfth to the fourteenth centuries as the lawless Middle Ages wore on, the populace was at the mercy of rival chieftains. The church was pledged to protect the weak;

together with a more humanistic promotion of decency and fairness. Thus Chivalry was born: the ideal was

> heroic character, combining invincible strength and valour, justice, modesty, loyalty to superiors, courtesy to equals, compassion to weakness, and devotedness to the Church.[29]

The knight (only youths of family and fortune need apply) attended his sovereign in times of war and in peace was at his sovereign's court, at banquets and tournaments, or traversing the country (as a knight-errant)

> in quest of adventure, professedly bent on redressing wrongs and enforcing rights, sometimes in fulfilment of some vow of religion or of love.[30]

The era of heraldry and pageantry

Heraldry refers to coats-of-arms (featuring emblems). Such were needed to distinguish participants in battles or jousts. Each coat-of-arms is defined by a *blazon* (a written description), so to draw it is to 'emblazon' it. A crest is a component of a coat-of-arms.

A medieval tournament is an example of a pageant. A pageant usually involved a richly costumed parade and a spectacular ceremony, or representations of scenes from history.

The beginnings of 'fashionable' melancholy

'Courtly love' became an offshoot of chivalry. Hunnish behaviour was off-limits for wooing the maiden of the castle (unless she was a serving wench), so, despite the feudal wars raging beyond the moat, the knight assumed a pale melancholy when in the presence of his lady, with his only aim being to please her and display his manly virtues. Sir Lancelot was the very flower of chivalry and also embodied the paradox of courtly love: such attachments were of necessity adulterous, as marriage was a political and business arrangement designed to cement alliances of families and nations.

> By late medieval or Renaissance times ... 'a man who suffered from that noble sensitivity, tristesse, or imitated Melancholia's pose' could hope to be admired for his intelligence (wit) and for the profundity of his mental concepts ... even empty-headed men pretended to be stricken with it.[31] BARBARA

No better than the howling of dogs

The church regarded minstrels, and indeed music other than church music, as allied with the Devil. The very location of minstrels' depiction outside cathedrals and churches, on the west wall – since night and demons come from the west – typifies this. Minstrels were excluded from the stratified social structure of the Middle Ages, and their music was accounted 'no better than the howling of dogs and wolves, without order ... a mess, chaos, muddled notions, the whole quite irrational'.[32] The main objection was to its purely secular character, and its lack of theological context.

In legends and fairytales the connection between Devil and minstrel is a favourite theme; for example, in Hieronymus Bosch's depictions of hell.

Music, melancholy and the Devil

Many tales recount how the Devil enters his victim so as to be able to shout or sing or cry from within him. Such possession could also take the form of melancholy, as shown by the Bible's account of David's harp-playing before Saul (1 Samuel 16:23).

Martin Luther accepted as perfectly real the exorcism of devils by the aid of (spiritual) music. He wrote:

> Music and theology alone are capable of giving peace and happiness to troubled souls. This plainly proves that the devil, the source of all unhappiness and worries, flees music as much as he does theology.[33]

Ideas of the demonic power of music reach well into modern times. Popular traditions preserve it in fairy tales and legends and, today, in customs such as the south German and Swiss Shrovetide celebration, marked by a cacophony of rattles, whip-cracking, bells, and pigs' bladders.[34]

> Thoughts of demons continued throughout the Middle Ages when Martin Luther wrote: 'All heaviness of the mind and melancholy comes of the Devil'. In other words, an external force was believed to be acting upon the hapless victim. The link between depression and hostility was not to be explained until 1917 when Freud, in *Mourning and Melancholia*, described depression as 'anger turned upon oneself'. Later in the century, depression came to be seen as a disorder of the brain. ELIZABETH

Miracle and mystery plays

Medieval Europe saw the development of the earliest plays, initially Bible stories or lives of the saints ('miracle' plays, performed in Latin and quite esoteric, and 'mystery' plays, accessible to all), accompanied by song and presented in churches. By the thirteenth and fourteenth centuries these had become more secular, and each craft guild (organisations uniting members of a trade) adopted a particular story from the scriptures. Some of the plays were particularly appropriate to the guild performing them, with the shipwrights performing the building of the

Ark, for example, and the bakers acting the Last Supper. During the fifteenth century mystery plays were set on decorated carts (*pageants*) and cycled around the cities on festival days.

Pontius and the black dog

An interesting Judeo–Christian source … may be apposite to our search for the 'black dog' fountainhead. This attribution arises from an ancient mystery play, *Pontius Pilate and the Jews* or *Pontius cum Judais*. One version is that the names of the puppet couple [Punch and Judy] were derived from the biblical figures of Pontius and Judas, who respectively were responsible for the condemnation of, and betrayal of, Jesus Christ. After Pontius Pilot had sentenced Jesus to crucifixion, the Roman governor of Judea was reputedly haunted for the rest of his life by a feeling that 'the evil one' sat on his back. Also, it is recorded that during Pontius' exile a black dog followed his every movement.

In the Punch and Judy folktale, Punch has a humpback affliction and is usually accompanied by Toby the dog. It is said that due to the flowing robe that he wore, Judas gradually became depicted as a woman, though a literal study of the mystery play's title suggests that this interpretation may be incorrect. The dog Toby's name apparently derives from the biblical reference to Tobias's dog … The sub-plot of Punch and Judy features an ultimately successful fight against ennui, disease, death and the Devil. KEITH

Readiness for the Renaissance

The ineffectiveness of the clergy in the face of the plague, the depopulation of the monasteries (the devout monks died tending the sick), and the influence of the French kings on the papacy, which they relocated to Avignon, fed a growing cynicism with the Church, and people began to entertain other styles of belief, and seek secular alternatives for their problems.

RENAISSANCE
CAPERS

The Middle Ages did not actually 'close', but evolved into the Renaissance (about the fourteenth to the sixteenth centuries). Curiosity about the world overcame fear, and religious strictures loosened. This cultural rebirth witnessed a human-centred and secular focus on art, literature and science.

Much can be attributed to a remarkable invention. In 1450 Johann Gutenberg, a German metal-worker and inventor, adapted the technology of wine and olive oil presses, using transferable metal type, to produce a printing press. Previously manuscripts had been transcribed by monks, or block-printed page by page with hand-carved text and illustrations.

By 1455, the printing press was enabling the mass publication and circulation of literature, science and ideas (and in languages other than Latin), together with a rediscovery of much of the literature of ancient Greece and Rome. A social revolution began, culminating in the Renaissance, as intellectual life moved from being the exclusive preserve of church and court, although Johann himself died in debt.

The tarot

Perhaps in reaction to the rapid changes ushered in by the Renaissance, Tarot cards – used for divination and as playing cards – became the mode. The cards are associated with mysticism and magic and carry images and symbols from Greek, Roman, Norse, Egyptian and Indian cultures. They have roots in alchemy, astrology and the Judeo–Christian mythology of sin, grace and redemption. From the fourteenth century they became popular for both game-playing and gambling (fulminated against by the Church). The *Arcana*, or 'hidden meaning', is very fluid, and tarot cards were (and still are) used for divination and to access the unconscious mind via symbolism and archetypes (*cartomancy*). The 'hermetic revival' of occultism in the 1840s saw Victor Hugo and others using them as a mystical key. They then became a staple of gypsy fortune-telling.

NOTHING MAN - DAVID FRAZER

Heartworm

> Hence, loathed melancholy
> Of Cerberus and blackest midnight born
> In Stygian cave forlorn
> 'Mongst horrid shapes, and shrieks, and sounds
>   unholy.
> – John Milton, *L'Allegro*

Melancholia, the female personification of melancholy, was a favourite theme of the artists of the late Middle Ages and the early Renaissance. ROBERT

The Renaissance ... derived from a French term meaning rebirth, was an era of scientific revolution and artistic transformation. During this period, an intriguing 'culture' of melancholic disposition arose in England in the early seventeenth century, largely due to the religious uncertainties instigated by the English Reformation, as well as a greater focus on the issues of sin, damnation, and salvation ... One of the most renowned writers to come out of the Renaissance, William Shakespeare (thought to be 1564–1616), made reference to melancholy in much of his work. SARAH

The dog: Melancholy's emblem

An emblem functions as a symbol or sign. It can be a distinctive badge, design or device, or an allegorical picture inscribed with a verse or motto presenting a moral lesson. Emblems were used frequently in illuminated manuscripts. They were also part of the Age of Chivalry, used by the knights on their coats of arms. Emblems exerted a fascination during the fifteenth to the seventeenth centuries.

[The dog] is a creature every bit as contradictory as Melancholy herself. It is also not the only animal, or even the most common animal, in Melancholy's menagerie; do not forget the owls, bats, nightingales and ravens that frequently attend her. BARBARA

In 1594, English poet Sir John Davies (1569–1626) saw the dog in a specific relationship with melancholy ...

> Thou sayest thou art weary as a dog,
> As angry, sick or hungry as a dog,
> As dull or melancholy as a dog ...
> – *In Cineam* DALE

When looking at the origins of the metaphor 'black dog', it is interesting to consider the work of the 'emblem writers' in the Renaissance period. Emblem books were a ... flourishing form of literature throughout Europe during this period, as writers drew upon fable, mythology, history, science and literature to represent abstract ideas in pictures and verse. Cesare Ripa's *Iconologia*, first published in Italy in 1593, portrayed 'melancholy' as a man wearing a dog's muzzle, resembling the silence and isolation felt by those suffering with depression. Another Renaissance emblem writer, Valerino, [showed] the dog, under [the emblem of] Saturn. In [Burton's] *The Anatomy of Melancholy*, an emblem depicts Saturn as the 'Lord of Melancholy'. DONNA

In Tilley's collection[35] it becomes evident that the use of the metaphor of a dog to describe melancholy, or depression, in Elizabethan times was clearly understood. SUZANNE

The melancholy anatomist

In the early seventeenth century, English culture was awash with sighs, dead lovers and general languishing.
GRAHAM

In 1621 Robert Burton's *Anatomy of Melancholy* was published, outlining fear, poverty and solitude as the causes of melancholy. By the eighteenth century, conditions such as hypochondria and other nervous disorders were noticed by the medical fraternity, and those with diagnosed melancholy, and enough wealth, tagged along to the European towns to 'take the waters'. Slowly, symptoms of depression such as anxiety, fatigue and discouragement began to be recognised, and by the nineteenth century, hypnosis became a popular tool for treating sufferers, leading to Freud's psychoanalysis ... in the twentieth century, finally to be replaced by drugs as scientific breakthroughs have revealed neurotransmitters in the brain.

Derived from the same etymology as 'melancholy', melanchetes, are, today, a species of labrador retrievers with black coats. JOANNE

In this aptly named 'era of reason and observation', we find in 1621 Robert Burton's *The Anatomy of Melancholy* heralding modern thinking. ANNE

Robert Burton (1577–1640) was certainly talking about the illness in his book ... because he declared he wrote the book to escape the ravages of this disease:

> Experience teacheth us that, tho' many die obstinate and wilful in this malady, yet multitudes again are able to resist and overcome, seek for help and find comfort, are taken from the chops of hell, and out of the devil's paws.[36] ALLAN

Robert Burton asserted that the causes of melancholia were

> either supernatural or natural. Supernatural are from God and his angels, or, by God's permission, from the Devil and his ministers. God permits the Devil to appear in the form of crows, and such like creatures, to scare such as live wickedly here on earth … for men's ministries, calamities, and ruins, are the Devil's banqueting dishes. BARBARA

Burton makes reference to numerous authorities on melancholia in this work, and points out that Agrippa and Lavater go so far as to assert that the melancholy 'humor' actively draws the Devil to it.

Selling your soul to the Devil

In the sixteenth century, during the witchcraft trials in Europe, the story of Dr Faust (or Faustus) spread through the Germanic regions. It was said that Faust, a physician who studied alchemy and the black arts, was pursued by a shape-shifting demon in the form of a black dog. Apparently Faust had 'sold his soul' to the demon in return for knowledge of the black arts and 24 years of life to enjoy them. JULIE

The Anatomy of Melancholy mentions Cornelius Agrippa, a fifteenth-century physician and occult philosopher from Cologne, who developed the reputation of being accompanied by a devil in the shape of a large black dog. Burton asserts that the devil was actually tied to the dog's collar. It was all nonsense of course, as Agrippa's pupil Johann Weyer, 'the founder of modern psychiatry', pointed out:

I knew that black dog very well when I was in Bonn. It was a dog of moderate size and his name was Monsieur, quite frequently when Agrippa was out walking, I would accompany him leading the dog on a rope.[37]

This case highlights, however, Christian society's [continuing] willingness, in the sixteenth and seventeenth centuries, to embrace the notion of demon familiars disguised as dogs (and as other animals). The legend of Agrippa's dog eventually made it into mainstream culture as the black poodle which transforms itself into Mephistopheles in Goethe's *Faust*. BARBARA

Witches get a reprieve

By the end of the sixteenth century, society came to its senses after several eminent doctors put forward theories that disproved the witchcraft myth. But this was not before a few of them became victims of the witch-hunt themselves. For example, the German scholar Heinrich Agrippa (1486–1535) analytically studied the various sciences of witchcraft (i.e. the occult, alchemy and astrology) and was able to speak out about the unscientific way that witches were judged. Unfortunately for Agrippa he owned a black poodle which was suspected of being his witch's familiar, but luckily he was able to refute the accusation and escape being tried. JULIE

That doggone melancholy

Of all other, dogs are the most subject to this malady, insomuch some hold they dream as men do, and through violence of melancholy run mad; I could relate many stories of dogs that have died for grief, and pined away for loss of their masters. – Robert Burton, *The Anatomy of Melancholy*

Burton also refers to dogs, black dogs in particular, as a subject for a person's morbid fear, paranoia, delusions or hallucinations, and records that black animals, including dogs, were associated with the demonic.

Melancholy multiplies

Several distinct kinds of melancholy could be distinguished in the course of the seventeenth and eighteenth century. Porter[38] identifies four different types: religious, intellectual, the outsider, and the melancholy of sensibility. Religious melancholy was a crucial concept in seventeenth century thought. Burton wrote on it at length: at its heart was the concept of original sin for which humans were punished over and over again, including through the means of melancholy or madness. For instance, hearing voices or speaking in tongues was not regarded as necessarily mad as it was to be in later times. KATE

Melancholy is the most eminent of the diseases of the phantasy or imagination; and dotage, phrensy, madness, hydrophobia, lycanthropy, St Vitus' dance and ecstacy are forms of it.

Burton [in *The Anatomy of Melancholy*] names the causes of melancholy as

the sine of our first parent, Adam … as our sins are the principle cause, so the instrumental causes of our infirmities are as diverse as the infirmities themselves … the greatest enemy to man is man, his own executioner, a wolf, a devil to himself and others.

He suggested two distinct types:

> natural melancholy, caused by an overabundance of black bile, and unnatural melancholy, a corruption of demons and spirits. MARCELLA

Out, bile melancholy!

Believe not these suggestions, which proceed
From anguish of the mind, and humors black
That mingle with thy fancy ...
– John Milton, *Samson Agonistes*

A doctor diagnosing [melancholia] would prescribe treatment to minimise the amount of black bile in the body or to increase the proportions of the other humors in relation to black bile – it was not primarily a psychological condition therefore, but a pathological one. From the sixteenth century, however, medicine was changing. Gradually, the links of 'melancholy' [to the humors] was replaced by an understanding of arteries and veins and circulation ... the popular meaning of the word 'melancholy' transmuted – the stimulus was a combination of the social use of 'melancholy' as a poetic frame of mind and the undermining of the classical system of medicine. GILLIAN

Melancholy was thought to be the result of an excess of black bile. 'Distemperature,' reports Burton, summarising a variety of learned sources [in *The Anatomy of Melancholy*], 'makes black juice, blackness obscures the spirits, the spirits obscured cause fear and sorrow'... The word 'distemper' belongs in this discourse because it has a human as well as canine form – it did, for a while, mean 'illness' ... We could, perhaps, popularise the word as an alternative for the lacklustre term 'depression', since distemper suggests someone whose 'temper' – read 'mood', 'spirit' or 'equilibrium' – is no longer temperate. JEFFREY

Sixteenth century author Timothie Bright wrote an important treatise on 'melancholy', summarising and describing it according to the science of the day … What we see in his *Treatise of Melancholie* is a clear balance between the intellectual, the poetic and the medicinal.

In this transition period, a cultural phenomenon also affected the idea of melancholy, where the appearance of it demonstrated refinement and aesthetic sensibility. The meaning of 'melancholy' influenced by this refined sensitivity, was sometimes softer and less agonising. One of the keys to the development of the softer, gentler form of melancholy … may have been its link to love. The special 'melancholy' of lovers had little to do with the balance of humors. It had everything to do with romance and popular culture. The melancholy of lovers was closer to the French *tristesse* than to the extremes of black bile. GILLIAN

Elizabethan England: The English Renaissance

The Elizabethan and Stuart world viewed itself as at the cutting edge of scientific knowledge: the English Renaissance was considered a golden age. Melancholy and depression were viewed as a social problem. From the early eighteenth century, symptoms became known as spleen, the vapours, hypochondria and hysteria. Richard Blackmore in 1725 classified the latter two as mental illness. The mentally ill were consigned to a closed world cut off from civilization and populated by outcasts as the insane took the place of the now less prevalent leper in leprosariums.

Though tolerance had increased, there were unusual ideas about treatment and management. It was at this period in European history that the local unemployable and oddities were put in a cart and transported out of their town to beg for a living. Others were consigned to the so-called 'ships of fools' under the care of mariners. These were sent to sea, travelling from port to port, in the belief that folly, water and sea had an affinity, that a sea change would somehow cure their own turbulence.[39]

> An early seventeenth-century cult of fashionable melancholia arose, perhaps a reaction to the dazzling culture of Elizabethan England. Melancholy was affec-ted by Russian aristocrats at the end of the nine-teenth century, as ennui or *toska*, meaning: melancholy, depression, yearning, anguish, pangs of love, tedium or nostalgia. ANN

Melancholia as the mark of a profound mind

A shift in attitudes between the Restoration and the Enlightenment was that 'the spirit kingdom' was losing its status as a cosmological reality, and was being aethe-rialised or turned to metaphor. [This enabled] the other form of melancholy – that of sensibility. This form of melancholy had broadly positive connotations.

Porter[40] offers an analysis wherein manics are seen to be paradigmatic of 'madness' or insanity; as somehow less or sub-human, terrifying and dangerous. By con-trast, images of the melancholic developed in quite a different way, and Aristotle wrote of the melancholy genius who was fired by 'divine fury' ... The creative genius, powered in part by melancholia, has a long his-tory prior to the Romantic era, and it was this concep-tion of the positive elements of melancholia that was to fuel the dual-natured aspect of depressive illnesses and experiences. This was later to develop into the 'melancholy of sensibility', an archetype used by writers, poets and artists from the eighteenth century onwards. KATE

[There were] more romantic notions of melancholy during the Renaissance period. The cultural and literary context of the Renaissance enabled the development of a broader view of depression that proposed a correlation between a depressive state and a profound mind. Indeed, Shakespeare's character Hamlet epitomised a sympathetic and thoughtful sense of melancholy which was antithetical to the anathema of the past. As a consequence, this new social and intellectual framework provided a means of challenging the dogmatic views of Christianity regarding depression. It was within this atmosphere that 'illness gradually overtook possession'.[41] FRANCES

In Elizabethan times melancholy was seen as a particularly English disease, and Harrison[42] and Babb[43] list many eminent Englishmen who were afflicted with bouts of melancholy, including Chaucer, Francis Bacon, Edmund Spencer and John Donne. PETER

Melancholy in art and music

The copper engraving of the goddess Melancholy by the artist Albrecht Durer (1471–1528) epitomises depression:

She sits not in an orthodox state of melancholic depression, but in a melancholy-induced trance, inspired by the daemon of Saturn, with her attention focused totally on the experience. The sleeping, and starved, dog beside her is indicative of the intensity of vision, with concerns of the physical world of senses left far behind; melancholy has been described as the sweet sleep of the senses.[44]

Symbols of the sciences of the time – alchemy and mathematics – lie around her, scattered and neglected.

During the sixteenth century melancholy continued in a favoured and familiar theme, with the melancholic

> ... a stock figure of tragedy, and even, sometimes, of comedy. He could be a malcontent, a rebel, or a scholar; he would be dressed in black, with a solemn visage, his arms folded and his eyes cast down. – Peter Ackroyd, *Albion, The Origins of the English Imagination*[45]

At this time, the term 'elegy' entered the English language and 'quickly acquired a peculiarly English tone: the lament is part of the tradition'. Ackroyd also refers to the

> long sweet note of pathos ... the plangent harmonies of Purcell and the stately threnodies of Spencer ... the funeral meditations of Donne and the lachrymose comedy of Sterne. ELIZABETH

Soft sorrow

The cultivation of the figure of the melancholic individual in Elizabethan and Jacobean England owed much to the madrigalists. The stock figure of the rejected lover, black-clad, spurning conviviality and wallowing in self-pity (as epitomised in Burton's *Anatomy of Melancholy*) can be discerned in a large number of madrigal texts of the period. The melancholic man was widely regarded as suffering a severe imbalance of the humors. For the composer, the challenge lay in extending the conceit of disharmony in the body by writing music which itself exhibited a lack of cohesion in one form or another.

The English ayre or lute song (turn of the seventeenth century) is a genre known for its inclusion of melancholic texts and sorrowful music. Melancholy's symptoms are imitated in its musical rhythm, mode and dissonance alluding to weakness, deformity, disharmoniousness and impropriety. It does not conform to the compositional rules of the time, using the lowered third (minor mode), called weak, womanly and submissive by theorists, and symptomatic of the downcast nature of melancholic; the metre continually changes, phrase lengths vary, and interior rhythms are syncopated or misaligned like a palpitating heartbeat: a common melancholic symptom. Rests constantly interrupt phrases, 'sighs' that mimic the melancholic's. Overall, the musical vocabulary consists of odd melodic intervals and harmonic dissonances, as well as chromaticism, indicating a lack of harmony.[46]

Melancholy and the music of the spheres

At the height of the Middle Ages ... there were current two very different concepts of the earth. The more popular was of the earth as flat, like a dish, surrounded by and floating upon a boundless cosmic sea, in which there were all kinds of monsters dangerous to man ... The more seriously considered medieval concept, however, was that of the ancient Greeks, according to whom the earth was not flat, but a solid stationary sphere in the centre of a kind of Chinese box of seven transparent revolving spheres, in each of which there was a visible planet ... the sounding notes of these seven ... made a music, the 'music of the spheres', to which the notes of our diatonic scale correspond. There was also a metal associated with each: silver, mercury, copper, gold, iron, tin and lead ... and the soul descending from heaven to be born on earth picked up, as it came down, the qualities of those metals; so that our souls and bodies are compounds of the very elements of the universe and sing ... the same song. – Joseph Campbell, *Myths to Live by*[47]

This reflected the Renaissance mystification of melancholy characterised by Robert Burton's *Anatomy of Melancholy*, and supported the notion of music as a cure for such an affliction.

Kepler, in 1595, found that the planetary velocities did correspond mathematically to musical intervals, and conceived of this pattern as producing ever-changing polyphonic chords and harmonies as the planets orbited around the sun. In Renaissance England, musicians were adjured by Stephen Gosson, a musician of the time, to 'shut your fiddles in their cases, and look up to heaven: the order of the spheres'.[48]

PAWS FOR ENLIGHTENMENT

From the seventeenth century on European thinkers broke away from the superstition and irrationality of the Middle Ages. This Age of Enlightenment (which includes the Age of Reason) believed in progress, and conceived the notions of capitalism and socialism (and the philosophies that led to the American and French revolutions). While religious belief and piety were valued, they were underpinned by the new rationalism, which also encouraged the empirical study of nature, the physical universe, philosophy and the developing sciences. The place and function of both church and state were questioned.

The birth of the blues

[The Enlightenment] gave rise to the idea that depression resulted from a failure to live within the rules of reason and natural law, however the Devil was still considered one of a number of possible causes including stars, old age, parents, diet, bad air and idleness (Robert Burton). By the mid-eighteenth century the causes of mental dysfunction were identified as moral irregularities or excess passions, and the responsibility shifted more to the individual.

The noun the 'blues' is recorded from 1741 and is a shortening of 'blue devils', which were thought to have been around since 1616. Such demons were popularly thought to cause depression and sadness.
DONNA

Self-conscious melancholy

Here rests his head upon the lap of earth
A youth to fortune and to fame unknown.
Fair Science frowned not on his humble birth,
And Melancholy marked him for her own.
Large was his bounty, and his soul sincere,
Heaven did a recompense as largely send:
He gave to Misery all he had, a tear,
He gained from Heaven ('twas all he wished) a friend.
No farther seek his merits to disclose,
Or draw his frailties from their dread abode,
(There they alike in trembling hope repose)
The bosom of his Father and his God.
– Thomas Gray, *Elegy Written in a Country Churchyard*

Quotes from Fielding's *Tom Jones* and Walter Scott's

Ivanhoe illustrate [how] morbidity is replaced by an often self-conscious soft sorrow and pensive sadness. Also Keats represents the gradual movement from clinical depression to light, romantic sorrow ... For a long time the two meanings (one with a medical underpinning, one more aesthetic) worked in tandem. John Milton used them both: 'Most musical, most melancholy'. So did Samuel Johnson. By the middle of the nineteenth century, it was almost impossible to use 'melancholy' without some sort of additive if the writer wanted to indicate that it was not an emotional state but something more serious. Charles Dickens, in *Hard Times* [1854]:

> The piston of the steam-engine worked monotonously up and down, like the head of an elephant in a state of melancholy madness. GILLIAN

The Renaissance fascination with melancholia and its association with 'sensitivity' ... may have persisted into the nineteenth century, for example in Keats' *Ode on Melancholy* (1820):

> She dwells with Beauty – Beauty that must die;
> And Joy, whose hand is ever at his lips
> Bidding adieu; and aching Pleasure nigh,
> Turning to poison while the bee-mouth sips:
> Ay, in the very temple of Delight
> Veil'd Melancholy has her sovran shrine,
> Though seen of none save him whose strenuous
>   tongue
> Can burst Joy's grape against his palate fine;
> His soul shalt taste the sadness of her might,
> And be among her cloudy trophies hung.
> ROBIN

Melancholy and the beau monde

Boswell [1740–1795], who wrote a newspaper column under the pseudonym The Hypocondriak [defined as 'that which produces melancholy'; also fashionably known as 'the English malady'], suggested that it was the done thing amongst the *beau monde* to develop depression because its sufferings were the hallmarks of a beautiful soul, proofs of superior sensibility. EVAN

– MATTHEW JOHNSTONE

Boswell's depression was quite a different animal to Johnson's. Although undoubtedly real and deeply felt, it had an element of self-indulgence that was becoming fashionable in that era. ADAM

Boswell's attitude was described in the context of his age:

For certain of Boswell's contemporaries, self-absorbed dejection was in vogue as a badge of identity. The Augustan generation of Swift and Pope had satirised lunatics, but by Johnson's day sentimental and sympathetic attitudes were gaining ground, making melancholy fashionable as the poet's affliction or the mark of refinement in a man of breeding. – Porter, 'The Hunger of Imagination: Approaching Samuel Johnson's Melancholy'[49]

This affectation was anathema to Johnson.

JOHNSON, BOSWELL AND THE DOG

Churchill, Johnson and Boswell, the famous trio whistled up by the metaphor of the black dog, have much in common, characteristics that go some of the way towards explaining their affliction. Dead, white Pommy males, all of them are literary gents – lest we forget, Winnie, astonishingly, won the Nobel prize for literature – and depression is part of the wages of creation. To a man they were overweight over-achievers who drank to excess, smoked and suffered from various dropsies and poxes and gouts. It would seem none of them much liked dogs [actually Winnie was devoted to his poodles – Ed]. Sam was passionate about cats, particularly his beloved Hodge whom he immortalised. Winnie warmed to pigs, observing that 'cats look down on us, dogs look up to us, pigs are our equals'. Jimmy was a gourmand who would probably have eaten any beastie with the right sauce. No doubt all of them were familiar with the homeopathic remedy of the hair of the dog, of whatever colour, that could enable them to jumpstart the long day's statecraft and/or letters through which they tried to prove themselves to the mother by whom they were neglected. OTIS

The origin of the species

We can pinpoint an almost exact moment when Dr Samuel Johnson crystallised the metaphor of the black dog, meaning melancholia. That he drew on the long history of association between the black dog and evil spirits and bad omens is certain. That he wasn't the first person to make this association is also probable. Nevertheless, it is fitting that England's greatest lexicographer should have given us the name with which we can recognise such a debilitating condition, and perhaps thereby get a hand on the black dog's collar. PETER

In its sense of 'depression', the term was certainly alive in the late 1700s. Samuel Johnson, one of the best-known English dictionary writers, was affected by a persistent depression. He knew the black dog, and so did his biographer, James Boswell. In a letter to Boswell on 7 November 1779, Johnson referred to

Boswell's depression when he asked 'What will you do to keep away the black dog that worries you at home?' a phrase echoed almost word-for-word by [Sir Walter] Scott in his 1826 quotation. BERNADETTE

The term 'to worry' was still used at that time in the sense of to tear or mangle, harass or persecute. It was later that it was used to denote the state of mind of a person 'worried' by their thoughts.

Not in the dictionary

Johnson suffered the black dog all his life, which makes it all the more interesting that he did not include the expression in his splendid *Dictionary of the English Language*, published in 1755. The modern sense of depression is covered there by 'melancholy' – 'diseased with melancholy' or 'habitually dejected' – just as the *OED* later defined 'black dog' as 'melancholy'. BERNADETTE

Two atrabilious authors

Boswell, in his biography of Johnson, tells us that his friend had his first major occurrence [of depression] when he was only twenty. He believed it likely that Johnson inherited this disposition from his father, who also suffered from melancholia. Boswell writes insightfully of the difference between depression with and without psychotic features, when he talks about severe melancholy making sufferers believe that their delusions are true. He writes compassionately about Johnson's fear that he will go mad, but also alerts us to how much insight Johnson had into his illness. Johnson wrote about his depression in Latin and presented it to his local physician and god-father, Dr Swinfen, as a case worth studying from a medical viewpoint. JENNY

Boswell described how the condition affected Johnson when he wrote:

> The 'morbid melancholy,' which was lurking in his constitution … affect[ed] him in a dreadful manner … He felt himself overwhelmed with an horrible hypochondria, with perpetual irritation, fretfulness, and impatience; and with a dejection, gloom, and despair, which made existence misery. From this dismal malady he never afterwards was perfectly relieved; and all his labours, and all his enjoyments, were but temporary interruptions of its baleful influence.[50]

Who would not feel for a man in such a sad state? BERNADETTE

Boswell … wrote of Johnson's elaborate sorrow, cult of remorse and the madness he suspected lay always just around the corner – 'fending off with cups of tea; attacks of the "Black Dog" of melancholy'. Johnson was obsessed with buttons, and had black dogs engraved on them, signifying melancholy, '… for without buttons we are all undone', he said. GREG

Johnson's self-help remedies

One of Johnson's favourite [books] was *The Anatomy of Melancholy* by Robert Burton, a seventeenth-century book dealing with the aetiology, symptoms and cures of depression. Johnson said it was the only book that ever took him out of bed two hours sooner than he wished to rise.

Johnson, who could use his wit, intelligence and

diligence to achieve many things in life, felt great distress at his inability to control his episodes of depression. It is not surprising that he would find metaphors likening melancholia to an outside force with a life of its own. How else could he explain these sudden changes of mood? Depression referred to as a 'black dog' and 'the demon melancholy' appears in the letters of Boswell and Johnson. They give and receive advice on treatments that wouldn't be out of place in contemporary psychiatry. Read and study (for these two men that is the equivalent of the cognitive behavioural strategy of 'scheduling a pleasurable activity'), never relinquish hope ('challenge any automatic negative thoughts') and exercise and get out in the sun. [Johnson] associates it with loneliness, and knows that distractions don't cure it but merely help keep it at bay for a short time. JENNY

Solitary nights were to be feared, for when darkness fell, the mind, like the eye, saw things less clearly than by day and confusions and perversions of the brain manufactured black thoughts. Which is why [Johnson] contrived to stay out into the small hours, to shrink the time left until the light came back.

> And then on Wednesday evening of the third week in April, climbing to his bed in Johnson's Court, he became aware of the Black Dog crouching on the landing, the shadow of its lolling tongue lapping the staircase wall. The stench of its hateful breath seeped into the chamber. He wrenched up the window to let in the night air, but still the rank odour swilled about the room; he propped himself upright and dozed with his hand clamped over his nostrils. – Beryl Bainbridge, *According to Queeney*[51] JOAN

A waggish observation

Like me, Johnson began suffering from depression as a teenager. Of course, in those days they didn't call it depression. Some called it 'the vapours', believing it to be caused by inhaling one's own burps. Others called it 'the disease of the learned', if for no other reason than to pander to the patient's ego. But the term which was in the widest use at the time was 'melancholy', a word derived from the Greek melan = black + kholie = a breed of sheepdog popular in Scotland ... Despite protracted and sometimes deep bouts of depression, Johnson led a productive life and died at the ripe age of 73. Death may have stopped him, but the black dog didn't. ROBERT

Still dogged by superstition

A black dog appears in Scott's *Ivanhoe* (1819) ... it was an incident alarming the 'superstitious Saxons' as the riders are leaving the monastery, 'the apprehension of impending evil' is a howling black dog, and the decision [is made] to turn back since – 'it is unlucky to travel where your path is crossed by a monk, a hare, or a howling dog, until you have eaten your next meal'. STEPHANIE

Other dog-wranglers

Johann Goethe wrote *Faust*, Part I in 1808 and *Faust*, Part II in 1832, based on a very early Christian legend, a previous version of which had been done around 1588 by Christopher Marlowe. A black poodle was the host of Mephistopheles (representing the Devil), who was challenging God for Faust's soul. VIVIENNE

Mephistopheles is derived from a combination of the Greek word for 'friend' (*philos*) and 'light' (*phos*) joined with the Greek negative (*me*), combining to give us 'not loving light'. ROBERT

Sir Walter Scott wrote:

> I was sorely worried by the black dog this morning, that vile palpitation of the heart – that *tremor cordis* – that histerical passion which forces unbidden sighs and tears and falls upon a contented life like a drop of ink on white paper which is not the less a stain because it conveys no meaning. I wrought three leaves however and the story goes on.[52]

Victorian poet Robert Browning (1812–1889) wrote of black dogs and death in his poem [*The Cardinal and the Dog*] (and also touched on melancholy):

A black dog of vast bigness, eyes flaming, ears that hung
Down to the very ground almost, into the chamber sprung
And made directly for him, and laid himself right under
The table where Crescenzio [the Pope's Legate] wrote –
Who called in fear and wonder
His servants in the ante-room, commanded everyone
To look for and find the beast: but looking they found none.
The Cardinal fell melancholy, then sick, soon after died:
And at Verona, as he lay on his death-bed, he cried
Aloud to drive away the Dog that leapt on his bedside. DALE

The depression of Honest Abe

Abraham Lincoln [1809–1865] is one of the more famous examples of persistence in the face of overwhelming odds and accompanying melancholy. His constancy ensured that he did not stagnate nor did he give up. Doris Kearns Goodwin relates how historians regard a broken off engagement to Mary Todd as the trigger to his famous depression, but it was his perceived failure as a politician, she maintains, that fed Lincoln's black dog. Many people believe that if he had not met such challenges and felt so utterly worthless at times he would not have achieved so much. DEBORAH

Abraham Lincoln was another statesman who achieved great things whilst struggling with depression. By all accounts of his temperament, being assassinated probably came as something of a relief to him ('Well apart from *that* Mrs Lincoln, how did the President enjoy the play?') GRAHAM

Mental health care

The ebb and flow of concepts and categorisations of melancholy and depression continued ... as science began to play an increasingly greater role, particularly during the seventeenth to nineteenth centuries. It was during the nineteenth century that the asylum system flourished. In addition to the dubious nature of 'health care' provided to individuals believed to be mentally unwell, such institutions were also reflective of the 'general alienation of late Victorianism'.[53] FRANCES

It would not be until the eighteenth and nineteenth centuries that a more rational and humane approach to those afflicted would result in the establishment of proper medical care, through the reformation of hospitals that previously had been dumping grounds for the mentally ill. MARTINE

OF SKULLS
AND ANIMAL
MAGNETISM

Is there no way of knowing
Where I have been, nor
Where I am going?
FRED CURTIS

The Victorian era (the eponymous Queen Victoria reigned from 1837 to 1901) is familiar to us in many respects. Tremendous changes occurred: the Industrial Revolution, then railways, steamships, the electric telegraph, newspapers and a trebling of the population. England became the richest nation in the world, though many working people lived brutal lives of near-slavery.

Hard times

By the end of the eighteenth century, the by-products of the explosion of factories and heavy industry were longer workdays, lower wages, widespread female and child labour, poor housing, disintegration of the family and little schooling. According to Klaus Doerner in his book *Madmen and the Bourgeoisie*,[54] 'malnutrition, fatigue and work accidents sent disease and mortality rates sky high. Alcoholism added its share in stunting lives.' CAROL

An era of opposites

Advances in health (the discovery of bacteria and antiseptics) and in science, most notably Darwin's theory of evolution

(1859), and great strides forward in the implementation of democracy, mass education, socialism and philanthropy, were coupled with a leaning towards sentimentality and romanticism, 'hyper-gentility', hypocrisy and superstition.

> In Victorian times [the crossroads still had] connotations of suicides and burials. The last known suicide to be buried at a crossroads [a tradition harking back to the goddess Hecuba/Hecate], after the jury returned a verdict of *felo-de-se* (self-murder), was Abel Griffiths, a twenty-two year old law student who murdered his father and then killed himself in June 1823. STEPHANIE

Widows' weeds and the cult of mourning

> Mark Twain [1835–1910] offers a comic view of [Victorian] melancholics through Huck Finn's encounter with the recently deceased, via Emmaline Grangerford. Her 'blacker than mostly pictures' (of mourning women at tombstones, beneath weeping willows) mock the execrable taste of the genteel middle-class, who mistook maudlin sentimentality for deep emotion. 'These was all nice pictures, I reckon,' says Huck, 'but I didn't somehow seem to take to them, because if ever I was down a little, they always gave me the fantods.' BARBARA

Emmaline illustrates an indulged emotionalism that was characteristic of the time.

Pseudoscience and spiritualism

People were torn between new materialism and old religiosity. Agnosticism and scepticism grew, but religious belief was valued, and most scientists and naturalists aimed to combine science and religion in a harmonious union. Doubt and the search for meaning fuelled the popularity of 'parapsychologies'. Spiritualism, phrenology and mesmerism became popular. Charles Dickens 'mesmerised' his wife, there is evidence that Queen Victoria attended séances, and a good proportion of the founding members of the new phrenological societies were medical men.

Parapsychologies offered all social classes the certainties of 'science', but within a Christian framework. Spiritualism came to Europe from America and offered, via mediums, séances and the ouija board a means of contact with the many souls who had not fared so well in the insanitary cities and hellish factories and had departed for, hopefully, better celestial climes.

In the late 1700s Johann Lavater, a Swiss priest, had linked facial traits to character. This was termed 'physiognomy', and set out principles concerning the human head. In fact, such observations prepared science for the theory of evolution. 'Phrenology', publicised as the science of the human mind, used the shape of the head to 'read' character. In fashion from the mid-eighteenth century to the late nineteenth century, it became recognised as quackery, and both phrenology and mes-merism were denounced by Ellen White (a prolific writer much noted at that time, and a founder of the Seventh-day Adventist Church) as 'Satan's means to destroy souls'.

Trees, and not a dog in sight

Mesmer, in 1778, theorised that there was a magnetic force common to all living things and which also influenced the celestial bodies and the earth. He demonstrated its curative properties by sitting patients around a large vat (*baquet*) filled with a mixture of unspecified substances. Each patient held a rod suspended in the liquid until the patient experienced con-vulsions, crying, laughter or other physical symptoms. Later,

Mesmer discarded the baquet and magnetised objects. Cures were claimed, for instance, when patients were tied to trees, due to trees' superior 'magnetic effluence'. The next development was a type of somnambulism, or transposition of the senses via 'animal electricity' or 'animal magnetism': a female patient walked through a town with her eyes tightly closed claiming to see from the pit of her stomach. The English fascination with electricity (current at that time!) provided a ready-made environment for mesmerism to become the vogue.[55]

Animal magnetism in action

A black dog encounter related by Charles Hardwick gives a literal demonstration of having a black dog on one's back:

> This tradesman, a Mr Drabble, assured my friend that the celebrated black headless dog-fiend, on one occasion, about the year 1825, suddenly appeared before, or rather, behind him, not far from the then Collegiate Church; and, placing its fore paws upon his shoulders, actually ran him home at a rapid rate, in spite of his strenuous resistance. He was so terrified at the incident that he rushed into bed in his dirty clothes, much to the surprise and dismay of his family.[56] ADAM

Melancholy sighs and black dog sulks

Melancholia appears at this time as 'nostalgia' (a term first used by a Swiss physician in 1688 to describe homesickness). Nostalgia was viewed as a 'disease', conflated or confused with melancholia, hypochondria and lovesickness, and believed to be more frequently displayed in those with superior sensibilities. During Victorian times illness was seen variously as self-indulgence, a clinical condition, sulky defiance (often referred to in this context as 'having the black dog on one's back') or superior sensibility.

> The general populace was clearly spooked by black dogs. They provided, therefore, a very useful bogey man or terrifying nursery metaphor. JDA Widdowson, who conducted a study in the 1960s into the kinds of animals used as threatening figures in systems of traditional social control, noted that dogs were predominantly invoked as threats against 'general misbehaviour' and that the majority of such dogs were 'big and black' and that it was usual to exaggerate the fearsome qualities of the animal. The black-dog-on-one's-back motif could not be described as a threat, exactly, but it does have a malevolent, warning aspect to it. Its purpose was clearly to invoke fear, or shame, and thereby to inhibit a depressed individual from 'sulking'. BARBARA

The archetypal Hellhound

> I am the wicked, lumbering dog in Sir Arthur Conan Doyle's *Hound of the Baskervilles*. I am the stealthy black dog of the night waiting to sap your life-force in Bram Stoker's masterpiece of gothic imagination, *Dracula*. I am an ominous presence in the gloom. HARRIET

>> A hound it was, an enormous coal-black hound, but not such a hound as mortal eyes have ever seen. Fire burst from its open mouth, its eyes glowed with a smouldering glare, its muzzle and hackles and dewlap were outlined in flickering flame. Never in the delirious dream of a disordered brain could anything more savage, more appalling, more

hellish be conceived than that dark form and savage face which broke upon us out of the wall of the fog. – Arthur Conan Doyle, *The Hound of the Baskervilles* VIVIENNE

Sherlock Holmes explains to Dr Watson how Winston Churchill might have come across the phrase 'black dog' ...

I believe Sir Arthur [Conan Doyle] first heard of Dartmoor's 'hounds of hell' [also known as 'wisht hounds': wisht means melancholy] in March 1901 on a golfing holiday in Norfolk, when the game was cut short by a storm. Their conversation turned to local myths ... the Black Shuck and other spectral hounds. It seems that while hiking over the moors with one Harry Baskerville as his guide, he met a neighbouring clan, the Vaughans, who owned a legendary huge, black dog. The haunting ruins and the moor's eerie weather created the perfect, ghostly atmosphere for his story, so bound up in local myth and legend.

Furthermore, Watson, I would like to postulate here that this book [*The Hound of the Baskervilles*] would have been a major influence on Churchill's use of the black dog in describing his depression. You see, Sir Arthur wrote about many other subjects than detective stories, and had varied interests, including fairies and magic. And many of his adventures are set between 1888 and the 1920s when Britain was at war. Churchill would have been *au fait* with the fact that dogs and war go back a long way. Ancient Assyrians, Persians and Babylonians; Romans; Attila the Hun – yes, yes, Watson – he used dogs called 'talbots', the ancestors of our very own bloodhounds, in his campaigns. Dogs defended caravans in the Middle Ages and Napoleon used them as sentries. Then there was Boots, that veteran dog actor of the 1940s, which helped raise more than $9 million in bonds to support the American war effort during World War II. In fact dogs have served in every modern war right up to the recent wars in Bosnia and Afghanistan.

Now here is the crux of my argument. Sir Arthur and Sir Winston both wrote books on the Boer War in 1900. They were so associated that they were featured together on a South African commemorative stamp in 2000. Winston was not only a contemporary of Conan Doyle, but they also kept up a vigorous correspondence. And note this, Watson, *The Hound of the Baskervilles* was first published in 1901! So they would both have been awash with black dog iconography.
ANNE

An additional note – Sir Arthur was a devoted student of Spiritualism.

Demon dog chases pandas

[The author Carol Rose has] recently been given anecdotes of otherwise inexplicable crashes of police cars on a dark empty road in Hampshire, which were ascribed to the appearance of the local supernatural Black Dog![57]
JOHN

Watson would no doubt have been interested to know about this.

And the malady lingers on

Robert Louis Stevenson [1850–1894] ... suffered from depression, and also Charles Dickens [1812–1870], another author of the time and sufferer of depression ... [Dickens is] referenced as a source of the quote 'let sleeping dogs lie' – leave those feelings of darkness at bay.

Honore de Balzac [1799–1850], a diagnosed depressive, also wrote of the Black Dog – 'All happiness depends on courage and work,' Balzac once said. 'I have had many periods of wretchedness, but with energy and above all with illusions, I pulled through them all.' Balzac made reference to Black Dog as a term for depression in the novel *The Devil's Heir* – 'make the best of it, shake the Black Dog off your back, adjust your petticoats, laugh, I wish it.'

Hans Christian Anderson [1805–1875] suffered depression. Human associations with dogs and dogs as portents of doom are a recurring theme in his fairytales. His upbringing as a pauper was a source of perpetual and unresolved traumas that affected his later life and inspired his fairytales. As a child he was forced to work in the wash-house of a mental asylum for women and listen to the inmates' ramblings. He was torn between his love of the arts and parental pressure to start a trade and at 14 ran off to join the theatre as a ballet dancer, actor and playwright ... *The Snow Queen* ... refers to a dancing little black dog – 'What you relate may be very pretty, but you tell it in so melancholy a manner.' GREG

Gerard Manley Hopkins (1844–1889), Jesuit priest and mystic, was afflicted with depression:

> I wake and feel the fell of dark, not day.
> What hours, O what black hours we have spent
> This night! What sight you, heart, saw; ways you went!
> And more must, in yet longer light's delay.

John Stuart Mill (1806–1873) developed *utilitarianism*, an economic theory that aimed to foster the greatest possible happiness for the greatest number of people. Unusually for his time, he was not raised with any religious beliefs. At times Mills questioned his direction in life. In his autobiography he wrote:

> The end [that is, if all his dearest wishes came true] had ceased to charm, and how could there ever again be any interest in the means? I seemed to have nothing left to live for. [I] hoped the cloud would pass away of itself; but it did not.
>
> … my love of mankind, and excellence for its own sake had worn itself out.[58]

Two years later he read Wordsworth and found

> a medicine for my mind … [the poems] expressed, not mere outward beauty but states of feeling, and of thought coloured by feeling. From them I seemed to learn what would be the perennial source of happiness.

Leo Tolstoy (1828–1910) questioned the meaning and purpose of life:

> These questions demanded an answer with greater and greater persistence and, like dots, grouped themselves into one black spot.

> A black retriever figures in the story 'Sawdust and Sin' from *The Golden Age* by Kenneth Grahame [1859–1932]. The dog, characterised as 'the swift-footed avenger of crime', snatches the toy clown, Jerry, and runs off with him. Jerry is described as a 'sinner' of 'distinctly bad' reputation.

The Black Man had got Jerry at last; and though the tear of sensibility might bedew an eye or two for his lost sake, no one who really knew him could deny the justice of his fate.

In *The Good Companions*, JB Priestly [1894–1984] makes the additional connection between the black dog, low spirits and the demonic:

> He [Jess Oakroyd] was troubled by a vague fore-boding. It was just as if a demoniac black dog went trotting everywhere at his heels. KAREN

Man's best remedy: A cat

In modern, secular times, the dog has got lost and shrunk into a psychological cliché. One online shrink proffers an emblem of the inner conflict at the core of our being by replacing good and evil angels with two dogs fighting, one black and one white. The dog that wins is the dog that is fed the most – so starve out the black dog of negativity and give that good white dog a bone. Once-potent metaphors turn to bromide and give the suffering mind no succour. A suffering mind might do better applying to a poet than a doctor. To Baudelaire, for example, who said he had a cat in his head and was the better for it. Imagining and eye-balling this seraphic cat, from which came a deep soothing vibration, was to him a means of steadying his judgment, a source of inspiration. He found this a better remedy than hashish or absinthe, and it has got to be more effective than an internalised dogfight. OTIS

WOE - DAVID FRASER

AUSTRALIA: NEW DOGS, OLD TRICKS

The big men proclaim 'Black Dog' and we
all know what they mean, but my landlord
does not permit me pets (though
a blue-tongue nests somewhere in the bricks,
and a bearded dragon eats the dandelions
in the backyard, and a feudal magpie
claims regular tribute of grubs and worms,
and my choir wears robes of lorikeet
and crow and noisy miner).

The big men proclaim 'Black Dog' but
my bastard has nor legs nor claws nor
tentacles but is as surface-tensioned
as an amoeba meniscus, as prehensile
as the arachnoid trapdoor of a dream.
– Ross Clark, from *No Pets Allowed*

Dogs down under

One notable story from Australia perhaps provides evidence of the persistence of the black dog legend beyond its native Europe. In Picton, NSW, there is a wonderful historical graveyard attached to the beautiful church of St Mark. Within the churchyard, the ghostly form of an enormous dog has been seen – even on one occasion chasing people out of the graveyard.

Local legend has it that a priest once buried his pet St Bernard in the graveyard, and perhaps it is the ghost of this animal that haunts the graves. However, some of the older gravestones also reveal family names that originated from Cornwall. Could there be some folkloric connection between the well-known black dog legends of Cornwall and Devon, and this mysterious ghost from rural Australia?

As long as there is fear of the unknown, the black dog stalks.[59]

Picton, NSW: 'Boy attacked by ghost, says mother' … *The Sydney Morning Herald*, 7 September 2005.

Naming rites

On a bushwalk in the Blue Mountains …

Two hours later we reached the ridge between Mount Mouin and Debert's Knob and looked back at the vista below − Kedumba Valley, a tiny clearing like a small green lake. As we rested, our leader told us the story of Black Dog Trail and how it got its name. The route was an ancient pass of the Aborigine, connecting the Burragorang Valley (now submerged by the Warragamba Dam) and the Megalong Valley. Settler Robert O'Reilly was shown the ancient tribal pathway by Jingery, native of the Gundungurra tribe … reciprocating for O'Reilly's help in applying for a land grant for him (this later forfeited when authorities found out who it was for). Having reached the ridge after the strenuous climb, O'Reilly is recorded to have said to Jingery … 'This is a black dog of a mountain!' This remark later led to the whole area becoming known as the Wild Dog Mountains − each peak called a 'dog' and named by colour. JOAN

Oz artists and the Dog

Australian author Henry Lawson [1867–1922] suffered severely from ... depression. The illness [was fuelled by] the heartache and disillusionment he felt during childhood. The product of an unhappy marriage, young Henry would flee to the back shed with his 'black, shaggy dog' to escape the violence of his rowing parents. There he would clutch his 'four legged mate' closely, and cry his tears into its shaggy coat. The 'shaggy dog' featured in many of his stories. Henry Lawson never overcame his depression, later seeking refuge in alcoholism. HEATHER

A recent interesting use of the black dog is in Arthur Boyd's 1972 portrait of Manning Clark. The painting consists of a full-length figure of Clark in front of the bush, and sitting lazily behind Clark is a black dog with a gleaming red eye ... Boyd was known for his use of both classical and biblical myth ... Clark was a well-known sufferer of depression. KATE

At a reading in Australia in 2003, the Australian poet Les Murray said 'I used to have depression'. Used to have. What a statement of faith and certainty. When a poet says it like that, he's choosing his words carefully. 'You're gone', he's telling it. And he's looking us in the eye and saying, 'It can go'. It is an act of faith for him, a benediction for others.

> Every day, though, sometimes more than once a day, sometimes all day, a coppery taste in my mouth, which I termed intense insipidity, heralded a session of helpless, bottomless misery in which I would lie curled in a foetal position on the sofa with tears

leaking from my eyes, my brain boiling with a confusion of stuff not worth calling thought or imagery:
it was more like shredded mental kelp marinated in
pure pain.[60]   BERNADETTE

Les Murray found that the black dog taught him to use
'poetry as personal therapy':

> I'd woken amid my State funeral,
> nevermore to eat my liver
> Or feed it to the Black Dog, depression
> which the three Johns Hunter seem
> to have killed with their scalpels:
> it hasn't found its way home ...

In a quote from *Travels with John Hunter*, Murray
describes the mysterious exit of the Black Dog from his
life.   CLEA

That old black magic

'The dress that got tongues wagging and split a nation' ran a
headline in *The Sydney Morning Herald* of 7 September, 2005:

> It is the dress that fuelled a thousand ugly rumours – the
> simple black outfit, decorated with red ribbons and
> buttons, which falsely convinced so many Australians 25
> years ago that Lindy Chamberlain had killed her baby,
> Azaria. It has been donated to the National Museum of
> Australia. The dress divided Australia when Azaria dis-
> appeared from the campsite at Uluru (Ayers Rock) in
> August 1980 [reportedly dragged from the family's tent
> by a dingo]. Lindy Chamberlain-Creighton donated the
> dress – and 200 items connected with Azaria's death and
> her own subsequent trials – to the museum in 1993 ...
> and they have now put it out as an exhibition ...

Blood sport

A report headlined 'A scent of blood – and the hounds rush in for the kill' in *The Sydney Morning Herald* of 1 September, 2005, about the resignation (and subsequent suicide attempt) of New South Wales ex-Opposition Leader John Brogden, quotes author and academic, Rod Tiffen, as saying that political journalists are 'either at the feet of politicians or at their throats'. The phrase, and the headline, highlight an ambivalence about man's best friend (dogs, not journalists!).

CHURCHILL:
THE BRITISH
BULLDOG

Winston had a large black dog
It followed him about
While Winston slept
It chased his dreams
Or lay there round and stout
It licked his face
It bit his hand
It growled
It snarled
It smelled
It gnawed away at Winston's faith
In God
In man
In self.
– peterxbrown, *Black Dog*[61]
Poem found by GREG

A master of the language

All babies look like me ... But then, I look like all babies. – Winston Churchill

When the US Congress voted to confer honorary American citizenship on Churchill in 1963, President Kennedy said, 'He mobilised the English language and sent it into battle'.

In addition to depression, another trait Churchill shared with his predecessor, Dr Samuel Johnson, was a gift and a flair for nomenclature. Churchill named the two wars the First World War (replacing the term 'Great War'), and the Second World War, renamed '[aeroplanes]' as 'aircraft' and 'aerodromes' as 'airfields'. 'He knew', as the writer Eliot Cohen remarked, 'that men are ruled by words'. VALERIE

Churchill's quick wit was legendary, and many of his sayings are available on the World Wide Web. A familiar one is his rejoinder to a fellow member of parliament, Lady Nancy Astor, who once remarked: 'Winston, if you were my husband, I'd put arsenic in your morning coffee'; to which Churchill replied: 'Madam, if you were my wife, I'd drink it'.

Vulnerability to the black dog

Like many children of the aristocracy, the new-born Winston [premature, and with a 20-year-old mother] was handed to a wet nurse, and soon after placed in the care of a nanny [much-beloved Mrs Everest, 'Woom', who died when he was 20] while his mother, Lady Randolph Churchill, resumed her fashionable social life. Nor was his father interested in Winston, and the ... unfortunate child was packed off to a boarding school at the tender age of seven. [Anthony] Storr[62] suggests that this early paucity of interest and affection had a long-term effect, depriving him 'of the inner source of self-esteem upon which most predominantly happy persons rely' ... How might Winston have dealt with this? One of his most obvious traits was that of extreme ambition. This included an element of fantasy, that took 'the form of a conviction that one is being reserved for a special purpose'. Storr also sees Winston holding depression at bay with work, a strategy that fell in a heap when he was out of office, or when one of his grand schemes failed (as with the Dardanelles campaign), deepening his depression. But worse was to come in old age, when 'the Black Dog finally overcame an old man whose brain could, because of an impaired blood supply, no longer function efficiently.' ELIZABETH

To Churchill the black dog was a potent symbol not only of the darkness to which it subjected his mind, but also of an unshakeable presence that, he believed, had pursued him along the bloodline from previous generations. Churchill's father, Sir Randolph, had suffered from deep depression that had worsened through his life and ended in insanity by the time of his premature death at the age of 46. Tragically, Winston probably never knew the true cause of his father's affliction and ultimate demise as it was to come to light after both their deaths in a letter written by Sir Randolph's neurologist: Churchill senior had suffered not from hereditary mental illness as Winston had believed, but from progressive deterioration due to syphilis. TIM

Churchill's black dog

Winston Churchill famously referred to his gloomy periods as his 'black dog', and many assume that it was another original contribution to English by the 1953 literature Nobel Prize laureate, succinctly characterising his relationship with depression. But he was, in fact, citing none other than his beloved childhood nanny, as related by his private secretary, John Colville. PAUL

Churchill's struggle

The term 'black dog'

> implies both familiarity and an attempt at mastery, because while that dog may sink his fangs into one's person every now and then, he's still, after all, only a dog, and he can be cajoled sometimes and locked up other times.[63]

> Churchill did not like to stand near railway platforms or wharves and even admitted that he disliked sleeping near a balcony – 'I've no desire to quit this world', he said with a grin, 'but thoughts, desperate thoughts come into the head.' – Storr, *Churchill's Black Dog, Kafka's Mice and Other Phenomena of the Human Mind*

Lady Soames – Churchill's only surviving daughter – was asked by Naim Attallah (Clementine Churchill's biographer): 'Did your father ever despair?'

Lady Soames:

> He himself talks of his black dog, and he did have times of great depression, but marriage to my mother very largely kennelled the black dog. Of course, if you have a black dog it lurks somewhere in your nature and you never quite banish it; but I never saw him disarmed by depression. I'm not talking about the depression of his much later years,

because surely that is a sad feature of old age which afflicts a great many people who have led a very active life.[64] VIVIENNE

Attempts at control

In one of the many instances where he uses that familiar term, [Churchill] speaks of being interested in consulting the doctor of his cousin's wife in case … 'my black dog returns. He seems quite away from me now – it is such a relief. All the colours have come back into the picture'. In another he speaks despairingly of 'the black dog that follows me everywhere.' Ironically, Churchill was also born in the Year of the Dog in the Chinese astrological charts, in the year 1874. People born in the canine years of the twelve-year cycle are supposed to be prone to depression if things do not go well. ELAINE

To avoid an immobilised state of misery, Churchill denied himself rest or relaxation, thus accomplishing more than most people just because he could not afford to stop. The fascinating ABC television series *Altered Statesmen* revealed Sir Winston Churchill as a driven, narcissistic individual who needed to be over-occupied to stave off his Black Dog. At times maudlin and drunk, Churchill's tragic last years when he had little to do are a sad conclusion to a great politician's life.

He invented various modes of coping with the depression which descended when he was no longer occupied by affairs of state, including painting, writing, and bricklaying; but none of these were wholly successful … in spite of the eulogies, the accolades, the honours,

Winston Churchill still had a void at the heart of his being which no achievement or honour could ever completely fill. – Storr, *Churchill's Black Dog, Kafka's Mice and Other Phenomena of the Human Mind*
GILLIAN

[Churchill] … became quite accomplished [at painting, selling] four pieces of his work at a Paris auction. His works seemed to reflect his mood: wide vistas of seascapes under a turbulent-looking sky, which nonetheless exhibited pockets of sunshine, peeking through the dark clouds. The visual essay of contrasting dark and light colours seemed to say that despite the dark clouds of despair, there was a ray of hope behind the bleak façade. Just wait for the stormy weather to pass. Just wait for the black dog to drop its guard.
CALVIN

The end of the chase

Then I went home happy and hungry, had a big steak then spent a few days finishing the lengthy but interesting *Life of Samuel Johnson* [by James Boswell], finding no black dog that Churchill might've noticed … but since Samuel Johnson's and Hester Thrale's more obscure letters and journals that do mention the black dog were read mainly by Johnson scholars until more widely published well into the twentieth century, Winston very likely first heard of the black dog when Woom [his nanny, Mrs Everest] sicked it onto his sulky back, or perhaps when feeling a bit low, she used the metaphor to describe her depression … MAX

THAT
FLAMING DOG
IS BACK

'Black Shuck', from the Anglo-Saxon *scucca*, meaning 'demon', was a 'large black hellhound, the size of a calf, with flaming eyes'.[65]

Literature, film, music

Pottering with intent ...

As we hungerers and thirsters after knowledge ... paw and snuffle (excuse the allusion) through their tales of Barquest, Black Shag, Guytrash, Padfoot, Hairy Jack, Hooter, the Gabble Retchets, the Gurt Dog, Devil's Dando, the Moddey Dhoo and, of course, Pooka in our search for the definitive truffle (this may not be as silly as it sounds; Harry Potter, who has transmogrified dross into gold — and thereby banished any lurking depression — for his creator, has recently been called upon to deal with 'Sirius Black', an 'animagus' who assumes the form of a, you guessed it, a Black Dog).
GRAHAM

The Grim is the omen of death and comes in the form of a large black dog which Harry unfortunately has turned up in the tea-leaves of his cup...

In [the children's book] *The Neverending Story* the coming of the great nothingness [is] signified by Glamork, a sinister black wolf who growls 'people who have no hopes are easy to control.' RUPERT

Writers around the world have offered hundreds of stories, first in literature and subsequently on film and television, detailing the special relationship dogs share with human beings. These include *Call of the Wild* (Buck), *Jock of the Bushveld*, *Dr Who* (K-9), *Turner and Hooch* and the eponymous heroes in *White Fang*, *Lassie*, *Rin Tin Tin* and *Benji*. EVAN

[There is an] exploration of the black dog metaphor in Ian McEwan's 1992 novel, *Black Dogs*[66] which suggests the folkloric myths served a social purpose, a means of giving form to collective sorrows, just as the metaphor for individual depression gives definition to this, until recently, misunderstood affliction. An encounter … becomes the defining moment in the novel. Bernard's wife June turns a corner in a French country lane, encounters two black mastiffs, has an epiphany and drives them away. Her tale subsequently becomes 'family lore, a story burnished with repetition, no longer remembered so much as incanted, like a prayer got by heart'.

Bernard says, 'You can forget all that nonsense about "face to face with evil". Religious cant. But, you know, I was the one who told her about Churchill's black dog. You remember, the name he gave to the depressions he used to get from time to time. I think he pinched the expression from Samuel Johnson. So June's idea was that if one dog was a personal depression, two dogs were a kind of cultural depression, civilization's worst moods.' CONAN

In her novel *The Holiday*,[67] Stevie Smith reflects:

Did Mama have these black dog moods when she did not hate anybody so much as herself, and not the devil more? What is the dog within us that howls against [happiness], the dog that tears and howls, that is no creature of ours, that lies within, kennelled and howling, that is an alien animal, and enemy? It is the desire to tear out this animal, to have our heart free of him, to have our heart for ourselves and for the innocent happiness, that makes us cry out against life, and cry for death. ANN

[The Black Dog] is still padding on down through the new millennium. For instance, in a recent film actually entitled *Black Dog*, actor Patrick Swayze has to overcome human predators only to come face to face with the 'Black Dog', the source of his personal demons. ANNE

And popular musicians compose songs about black dogs, as pointed out by Evan, who cited the Manic Street Preachers' *Black Dog on my Shoulder* and Chris Rhea's *Black Dog*; while Tim found a Nick Drake song called *Black Eyed Dog*.

Nick Drake overdosed on antidepressants and died in November 1974.

RECOVERY FROM THE BITE

The condition you're in can't get very much worse
perhaps all will end with a ride in the Hearse ...
... you are having another so-called Blackdog day
won't last long, I hope and I pray
but the mood lingers on, takes time to wear off
got to run its course, just like a cough ...
ROBERT APPELBY

The black cloud

Gordon Parker, Executive Director of the Black Dog Institute, notes that people often describe their depression as having 'black' connotations; and, interestingly, some only see 'colour' when their depression lifts.

Black ... symbolises

> Primordial darkness; the non-manifest; the void; evil; the darkness of death; shame; despair; destruction; corruption; grief; sadness; humiliation; renunciation; gravity; constancy.[68]

Others have proposed that the association of darkness with negativity or pain is an inbuilt human mechanism, that depression has been represented cross-culturally in black, and that the notion of a black mood is amply established in Homer [c.700 BC], who describes 'a black cloud of distress' such as affected the depressive Bellerophon. CLEA

Black has been part of many a metaphor for various medical diseases, which are usually either fatal or very severe. Black cancer has been used to describe meningococcal meningitis, black pox is severe smallpox, and no medical metaphor is more famous than the outbreaks of the Black Death, when bubonic plague spread rapidly through large populations. Blue seems to have some nasty affiliations as well, with the blue measles and blue plague both referring to typhus, but I don't think that the connotations of blue are ever as bad as black. I would rather have typhus than meningococcal meningitis, and the blues are really a watered-down variant of depression. After our hearts are broken in love we wallow in sad songs for a bit before moving ourselves through the blues, but when the black dog descends we often require a good dose of psychotropic medication, counselling from health professionals and sometimes even a hospital bed. JENNY

The adjective 'black' and its many companions including: dark, dismal, dreary, sombre, murky, funereal, gloomy, shade and shadowy, or tropes like the dead of night, the witching hour and black as the pit (Hell), act as ideal references to a state of depression as well as reaction to thoughts on death and the unknown. Black is being enveloped in darkness; it signifies evil in art; as a mortuary colour it is grief, despair and death. A black cap was once worn by judges when passing the death sentence. Magic is the black art. There are black lists, black looks, blackmail, black markets and the Black Mass; Black Dog is another name for the blues ... FRED

The black cloud lifts

For those who have dwelt in depression's dark wood, and know its inexplicable agony, their return from the abyss is not unlike the ascent of the poet, trudging upward and upward out of Hell's black depths and at last emerging into what he saw as 'the shining world.' There, whoever has been restored to health has almost always been restored to capacity for serenity and joy, and this may be indemnity enough for having endured the despair beyond despair. – William Styron, *Darkness Visible* [69]

Recalling my recovery from depression I remember the relief I felt at finally being able to smile spontaneously at the sight of a colourful flower or parrot. While I was sick with depression my sense of smell and sense of hearing had become sensitised and my sight had dulled. Black is indeed a relevant and meaningful metaphor for the colourless world of the depressed individual. TERESA

For many the recovery phase is slow and tedious – full of trauma, hospitals, shock treatment – truly a dog's life – and black... VERY black – black as the ace of spades, the Black Hole of Calcutta, the Black Death, a Black Mass, blackwater fever, black as ink!! Ah yes – so easy to want yourself to 'black' out and get away from it all. JOAN

The words to say it

Black Dog howling
Black Dog growling
Black Dog creeping
Black Dog
Black Dog pouncing
Black Dog biting
Black Dog sleeping
Black Dog tearing you apart
Black Dog tearing out your heart
BLACK DOG, ELYSE NICOLLE HAMMOND

If ever the human psyche held terrible secrets, and untouchable emotions, the language of modern psychology has opened its dungeons and let those dark hounds loose. The ignorance that kept us mad and mute, has been replaced by a poetry of sorts. We now have words – and chemicals – that can hook those nameless demons, cauterise them, splay them and even neutralise them. Science and the language to delineate

it have for now rescued millions of listless, melancholic, insomniac, suicidal individuals from the grip of a condition Winston Churchill called 'the black dog'.
JOANNE

In good company

… listing some of the innumerable creative and gifted people who have been afflicted with depression or bipolar disorder, and quoting Francisco de Goya y Lucientes, the Spanish painter [1746–1828]:

> Fantasy, abandoned by reason, produces impossible monsters: united with it, she is the mother of the arts and the origin of marvels. GLAD

Enter the other colours

 Colours, like features, follow the changes of the emotions. – Pablo Picasso

I must say I like bright colours … I cannot pretend to feel impartial about the colours, I rejoice with the brilliant ones, and am genuinely sorry for the poor browns. – Winston Churchill, an accomplished painter

> White as innocence, black as evil, red as lust and green as envy – colours are often linked with emotions and carry moral implications. Mental illness has also been viewed through moral lenses, so it's not surprising that depression has acquired its own colour. JENNY

>> When I leave prison both the laburnum and the lilac will be blooming in the gardens and I shall see the wind stir the restless beauty, the swaying gold of the one and make the other toss the pale purple

of its plumes so that the air will be Arabia for me. I know that for me to whom flowers are part of desire, there are tears waiting in the petals of some rose. There is not a single colour hidden away in the chalice of a flower or the curve of a shell to which by some subtle sympathy with the very soul of things my nature does not answer. – Oscar Wilde, *De Profundis* – the book that he wrote while he was in prison DEBORAH

– MATTHEW JOHNSTONE

Peace rains

Golden days are rare,
Golden days are pure joy
Rolled gold.
Silver days are seldom,
Silver days are pure magic
Silver lined.
Purple days are few,
Purple days are pure inspiration
Deeply purple.
Black days come and go,
Black days are pure hell
Black dog days.
Clouds gather full of countless tears
Golden Silver Purple Black Tears
Spear the bloody Red stained earth.

JOHANNA

HERE ENDETH
THE TAIL

Since God said Let there be light! And He saw that it
    was good,
Darkness He condemned as bad: of course, that's
    understood;
And Dogs in human history go back and back and
    back,
And Dogs alone dog humankind – as Black alone is
    Black …
The Black Dog of Depression has dogged me all my
    life

Cheated me of livelihood, of family, of wife;
He runs in vicious circles, his chains my brains
    entwine,
He feeds upon his hateful self as he also feeds on mine.
So I am well acquainted with Black Dog, in many a
    guise;
The one that makes me despise myself is the one I most
    despise.
But Fie on Black Dog! I will laugh at him before I
    die,
And with envenomed poison pen, I'll do him in the eye!
BRUCE

Black Mutt: 'Best of the block'

From Winston Churchill there are lexicographical stepping-stones back to the origins of the term black dog for depression, perhaps as early as 856 AD in the Annales Franorum. English literary stepping-stones include figures such as Arthur Conan Doyle, Robert Louis Stevenson, Sir Walter Scott and Samuel Johnson to Bartholomew de Granville, the *Anglo-Saxon Chronicles* and *Beowulf* – almost a millennium of reference and suggestion of the black dog inhabiting troubled minds. The black dog crossed into English literature from English folklore and from there into a terminology for depression. This lore was based upon Celtic, Anglo-Saxon, Norman and Viking language and cultural influences: England's inhabitants and invaders. The black dog might just be a mongrel. SETH

It is ultimately unlikely that 'black dog' was a specific term for depression before Churchill used it, but was rather a vague reference to anything which rendered someone less than congenial, whether ill temper, fear, guilt or, indeed, melancholy; as recently as 1956, it was defined simply as 'peevish fit', especially in children. Other terms which also began their ascent in the eighteenth century – the 'blue devils' (1780s), 'the blues' (1740s) and more general descriptions of depressed spirits – were more frequently recorded, at least in published texts, and generally retained a more specific relationship with 'depression'. Adoption of 'black dog' by Churchill (and by those who write about him) thus represented a turning point for the beast; and once the adoption became public, whatever it was exactly that Churchill meant, 'black dog' could assume its now secure place in English as a metaphor for depression.

PAUL

The history of language and symbol … is never straightforward. To this point, I have attempted to follow an at times somewhat tenuous trail of breadcrumbs to examine the history of the Black Dog metaphor, to uncover its point of origin. I would contend, however, that ultimately, such a point does not exist, and that the evolution of the metaphor is better conceived of as a process of cross-pollination, a circulation of complementary discourses which feed into and inform each other, culminating in the specific image we have today, rather than as a linear process in which a single, identifiable 'original' usage develops and evolves over time.

[There is a broad] discourse which associates the figure of the dog with death and decay. The Black Dog of Bungay makes the direct reference to the

Black Dog being on a person's back ... but there is no explicit reference here to either bad luck or melancholy. The spectral black dogs of British folklore combine associations with the Devil and their ancient positioning as gatekeepers of the Otherworld to act as earthly omens of disaster. Each of these constructions emphasises a different aspect of the creature, and the combination of these operates in an inter-textual process to give the image of the Black Dog the range of associations it has acquired across its long history. To speak of a point of origin becomes moot, since the metaphor as we know it is the sum of all these parts, in complex relationship with each other over time. MEGAN

It has been a struggle to find the real Black Dog. If only he did look like Cerberus, his eyes, in all three heads, flashing like large red circles of fire, his jaws snapping ravenously, vile slather spouting wolf's bane as it splashes about, his tail whipping menacingly with its serpents writhing and striking. We might all find the strength of Hercules, the guile of Sybil or the musicality of Orpheus if he were to be so substantiated.

But our own Black Dog yet remains a mystery – true to the metaphor he is. Still a hunter of the sad, the grief-stricken, and the fragile. Still a hell-hound – a devil to shake off. Yet, remarkably faithful, loyal and persistent. Tame and beastly all at once. The wolvine canine shape-shifter. Depression. SUE

And so the image lives on, standing testament to the human need to give shape to the vagaries of mental illness. We have now chased the black dog from its distant origins in ancient superstition to its maturity as a metaphor for human depression. The quest for self-knowledge has seen writers past and present delve into this rich tradition of allusion to define aspects of the personality that resist control. In each generation, the black dog produces another litter of shadowy offspring; yet through understanding and empathy, this cycle can be diminished. Regardless, the black dog will never disappear in totality, for it is part of the complex mosaic that is the human psyche. REBECCA

I was interested to learn, after reading about Bill Clinton's quadruple bypass, that depression is one common side-effect of open heart surgery. Although he is someone who seems never to have been subject to bouts of depression before, it would be interesting to know if, sitting up in his hospital bed, chatting with Hillary about how he was going to give up fried chicken and hamburgers for lentil-burgers and skinless, boiled chicken (and feeling, as he speaks, a small, unfamiliar pit of depression forming in his stomach), whether he caught a fleeting glimpse out of the corner of his eye of something that reminded him of that piebald, rascally pup that nipped him on the ankle in Australia two years before; only this would be a much darker beast, black as melancholy and perpetually on the periphery of his vision, much harder to pin down than any ordinary dog, yet somehow always there. It's possible. But I can't imagine Bill Clinton's black dog lasting for very long, can you? DAVID

At the end of the day it is not important that we understand the derivation of the term 'black dog'; it is important, however, that we muzzle the creature. This we are learning to do with greater and greater skill and sensitivity. JEFFREY

As stigma persists – still with us but hopefully mortally wounded – people have had to find ways to reconcile their notion of weakness, moral failure or demonic mischief with the emergent facts of rogue biology. NEIL

As I write, my own pet black dog is at my feet. We have been together for more than ten years and are rarely apart. I chose her from the line-up at the RSPCA when I was in the middle of a spectacularly grim bout of depression. She seemed like a victim, harassed by the others at the pound and it was my job to save her. As soon as we arrived home, my new dog tore through the house, rolled over the grass, the furniture and us. I realised then I had been hoodwinked. But my dog is no longer completely black. Her muzzle has grown white, as have parts of her tail. This, I believe, is a neat metaphor. As I have learnt to tame my *black dog* over the years, my pet is also older, wiser and not prone to outbursts of erratic behaviour. I like to think we are both mellowing and appreciative of our allotted time. As Herman Melville says [in *Moby Dick*]: 'Thus sailing with secret orders, we ourselves are the repositories of the secret packet, whose mysterious contents we long to learn. There are no mysteries out of ourselves.' CAROL

And from the British Bulldog

We are all worms. But I believe that I am a glow-worm.
– Winston Churchill

SINCERE APPRECIATION FROM THE BLACK DOG INSTITUTE

The Black Dog Institute would like to compliment each writer on their illumination of some facet of the history or experience of depression, and begs indulgence for using selective quotes to fashion this kaleidoscope, rather than respecting the integrity of the writer's piece. There has been quite some anguish experienced as the wave of entries just simply overflowed the capacity of this vessel. I can sincerely say that every single piece had a lovely turn of phrase or an original insight and, in many cases, a heartrending and courageous story. Staff at the Institute have been privileged to have been a part of this exercise.

THE WINNING ENTRIES

When you curl, stuffed, in the pot at the rainbow's end
it is life roaring and racing and nothing you can do.
Were you really God you could have lived all the lives
that now decay into misery and cripple you.

– from *Corniche*, Les Murray

The three essays that follow, together with ten other highly commended entries, are posted on the Institute's website: <http://www.blackdoginstitute.org.au>.

FIRST PRIZE

'BLACK DOG'
as a metaphor for depression:
A brief history

PAUL FOLEY

Winston Churchill had a black dog
his name was written on it
It followed him around from town to town
It'd bring him down
took him for a good long ride
took him for a good look around.[1]

'Black dog' is a powerfully expressive metaphor that appears to require no explanation. The combination of 'blackness' with the negative connotations of 'dog', noun and verb, seems an eminently apt description of depression: an ever-present companion, lurking in the shadows just out of sight, growling, vaguely menacing, always on the alert; sinister and unpredictable, capable of overwhelming you at any moment. Further, the 'dark hound' is an archetypal object of fear, with a long tradition in folklore and myth. Black dogs in dreams are interpreted negatively, often representing death; from all over the world come tales of nightmares caused by oppressive black dogs crushing the sleeper's chest.[2]

Winston Churchill famously referred to his gloomy periods as his 'black dog', and many assume that it was another original contribution to English by the 1953 literature Nobel

Prize laureate, succinctly characterising his relationship with depression. But he was, in fact, citing none other than his beloved childhood nanny, as related by his private secretary, John Colville:

> Of course we all have moments of depression, especially after breakfast. It was then that [Lord] Moran [Churchill's doctor] would sometimes call to take his patient's pulse and hope to make a note of what was happening in the wide world. Churchill, not especially pleased to see any visitor at such an hour, might excuse a certain early-morning surliness by saying, 'I have got a black dog on my back today.' That was an expression much used by old-fashioned English nannies. Mine used to say to me if I was grumpy, 'You have got out of bed the wrong side' or else 'You have got a black dog on your back.' Doubtless, Nanny Everest was accustomed to say the same to young Winston Churchill. But, I don't think Lord Moran ever had a nanny and he wrote pages to explain that Churchill suffered from periodic bouts of acute depression which, with the Churchillian gift for apt expression, he called 'black dog.' Lady Churchill told me she thought the doctor's theory total rubbish ...[3]

Whatever the truth about his state of mind, the young Churchill evidently inherited 'black dog [on your back]' from Mrs Everest (born in the 1830s), albeit as a designation for ill humour in general, rather than depression.

'Black dog' in nineteenth century dictionaries

This is consistent with nineteenth century dictionary definitions. James Murray noted in the *New English Dictionary* (1888), precursor of the *Oxford English Dictionary* (*OED*), that 'in some country places, when a child is sulky, it is said 'the black dog is on his back';[4] in other places, the sulky child was the 'black dog'.[5] Farmer and Henley's respected dictionary of slang (1898) noted that 'black dog is a frequent figurative expression dialectically for depression of spirits, and melancholy',[6] and the abridged version also mentioned the 'sulky child',[7] while the *English Dialect Dictionary* (1898) recorded 'a fit of bad temper'.[8] At about the same time, the *American Century Dictionary* (1889) described 'black dog' as 'hypochondria; the blues',[9] expressions employed at this point to describe a spectrum of phenomena ranging from 'moodiness' to what we call 'clinical depression'. Finally, Chambers' *Book of Days* (1864) included an article on 'spectre-dogs', which commented that 'to have the black dog' on the back was a common phrase (without defining it), 'though perhaps few who use it have an idea of its origin.'[10]

At this juncture I should mention that 'black dog' has been used in many contexts irrelevant to our discussion: to describe guns, miners' lamps, prisons (the infamous Newgate 'Black Dog') and counterfeit silver coins; in unrelated phrases ('like butter in the black dog's house': Scottish = beyond all recovery); and as a general term of abuse. And to avoid another misunderstanding: 'black dog' has nothing to do with having a 'monkey on one's back', a more recent phrase which referred to mortgage debt, and more recently to any depressing burden, especially addiction.[11] All this noted, we can now investigate the pedigree of our 'black dog'.

Roman origins?

Brewer's authoritative *Dictionary of Phrase and Fable* (1894) included the following entry:

> A black dog has walked over him. Said of a sullen person. Horace tells us that the sight of a black dog with its pups was an unlucky omen.[12]

But what we actually find in Horace (65–8 BC) differs somewhat from Brewer's reading. In his *Carmina* (III, 27), Horace lists a number of unpleasant omens, including the sight of 'a pregnant bitch (*praegnans canis*) … or a vixen with young'.[13] It has also been suggested that Horace referred to the 'black dog' while discussing the illusion of freedom in one of his satires (II, vii):

No company's more hateful than your own:
You dodge and give yourself the slip; you seek
In bed or in your cups from care to sneak:
In vain: the black dog follows you, and hangs
Close on your flying skirts with hungry fangs.[14]

Horace is not speaking here of melancholy; but more importantly the Latin text does not mention a 'black dog', but rather *comes atra*, or 'dark companion'. A more appropriate translation would thus be: 'the dusky companion presses upon you, and follows you in your flight.'[15] Horace would thus appear to be a red herring.

Both the standard reference on all aspects of antiquity, Pauly's *Realencyclopädie*, and its recent revision, *Der neue Pauly*, include extensive discussions of dogs in the ancient world, including the belief that encountering a black dog was inauspicious,[16] and that howling, black or pregnant dogs could also be significant.[17] The comprehensive discussion of canine superstitions in Latin literature by Eli Edward Burriss [18] also records a fascinating range of beliefs, but nothing relevant to our term; the same is true of other authoritative accounts of the animal symbolism in the ancient world.[19] Further, I have been able to locate only two other places in Latin literature even faintly relevant to our 'black dog': in *Phormio*, Terence (190–59 BC) lists amongst other prodigies 'a strange dark dog (*ater alienus canis*) entering the house' (IV, 4), while his fellow comedian Plautus (250–184 BC) wrote in *Casina* (V, 4) of a 'dog omen (*canina scaeva*)', from the Roman idiom 'between the wolf and the dog', equivalent to our 'rock and a hard place'.

There are certainly many classical references to black dogs as underworld denizens (Anubis, Cerberus, Hecate's hounds), but black dogs were also highly prized by our Roman forebears as guard dogs and for their healing powers.[20] None of this, however, explains our 'black dog', nor do beliefs concerning the Dog Star (Sirius) and the languid 'dog days' of high summer. It is interesting, however, that lycanthropy, the ability to assume the shape of a wolf, was long regarded as a form of melancholia.[21]

Medieval and early modern periods

During the Middle Ages, the dog represented a variety of qualities, including melancholia – hence the dog in Dürer's *Melencolia I* (1514) [22] – but primarily more positive characteristics: companionship, faithfulness, bravery, intelligence.[23] Although it is true that they often figured as companions of devils or witches, as malevolent apparitions ('fetches') projected by practitioners of the black arts, and the 'Devil [was] frequently symbolized by a black dog',[24] medieval dogs were generally seen in a positive light. At the end of the sixteenth century, however, dogs do appear in proverbs as melancholy creatures:

> … as malincholy as a curre dog, according to the Bysshopricke proverb. (1592)

> I'll be very melancholique, i' faith. – As a dog, if I were as you, sir John. (1616) [25]

But this association is probably less symbolic than reflective of real dogs, as we read in Robert Burton's monumental treatise, *The Anatomy of Melancholy* (1621):

> Of all other [animals], dogs are most subject to this malady, in so much, some hold they dream as men do, and

through violence of melancholy, run mad. I could relate many stories of dogs, that have dyed for grief, and pined away for loss of their masters ...[26]

Burton's tome, a thorough consideration of the various forms of melancholy but also a masterpiece of English literature, included a few other pertinent passages:

Montanus ... speaks of one that ... dares not venture to walk alone, for fear he should meet the devil, a thief, be sick; fears all old women as witches, and every black dog or cat he sees he suspecteth to be a devil ...[27]

The last main torture and trouble of a distressed minde, is ... Gods heavy wrath, a most intolerable pain and griefe of heart seizeth on them ... they smell brimstone, talk familiarly with divils, hear and see chimeras, prodigious, uncouth shapes, bears, owls, antiques, black dogs, fiends, hideous outcries, fearful noises, shreeks, lamentable complaintes ...[28]

[Papal Legate] Cardinal Crescence died likewise so desperate at Verona [after the Council of Trent, 1552], still he thought a black dog followed him to his death-bed, no man could drive the dog away.[29]

The latter story was well-known via reports in compilations of historical wonders and books on dream interpretation. A large black dog with flaming eyes had entered the cardinal's chambers, but could not be detected by his servants; the cardinal thereupon fell into a 'melancholy', and died shortly afterwards.[30] This 'black dog' was thus associated here more specifically with pangs of conscience and fear of divine punishment than with melancholia itself. Not that the depressed are strangers to fear and guilt, but the 'black dog' at this stage was more a harbinger of doom than a long-term companion.

As late as the second half of the eighteenth century, beliefs that black dogs (like black cats) were evil omens were still pervasive, as reported in a magazine article concerning rural superstitions:

> ... but a pin with the head turned towards you, or to be followed by a strange dog, I found were very unlucky.[31]

But we find little trace of the gloomy hound in other literature. Shakespeare portrayed many memorable melancholics, but his only reference to a 'black dog' involved the metaphor for shamelessness (1594):

> First Goth: What! canst thou say all this, and never blush?
> Aaron: Ay, like a black dog, as the saying is.[32]

Almost a century later, we meet the following in a burlesque play, but this, too, was an isolated example:

> Why frowns? my beautious dear,
> Thy Forheads muffl'd in black pouts,
> Like warlike Steed in Fun'ral clouts ...
> But strait in black dog'd masters Course
> My dear looks sad as morning Horse.[33]

Samuel Johnson and Mrs Thrale

But then we discover a series of citations which associate 'black dog' with Samuel Johnson, compiler of the first major English dictionary and inveterate letter writer. One correspondent, the colourful Mrs Hester Thrale (1741–1821), appears to have been the first to mention it (16 May 1776):

> Mr. Thrale, thank God, is very comfortable set up again. The last gale blew him almost down though ... but he scorns the black dog now: he will swing him round and round soon as Smollet's heroes do ...[34]

Johnson wrote on 31 October 1778:

> Long live Sir John Shelly, that lures my master [Mr Thrale] to hunt. I hope he will soon shake off the black dog, and come home as light as a feather.[35]

Mrs Thrale replied:

> I have lost what made my happiness in all seasons of the year; but the black dog shall not make prey of both my master and myself ... My master is a good man, and a generous, he has made me some valuable presents here; and he swims now, and forgets the black dog.[36]

This elicited Johnson's dual responses:

> I shall easily forgive my master his long stay, if he leaves the dog behind him. We will watch, as well as we can, that the dog shall never be let in again, for when he comes the first thing he does is to worry my master. This time he gnawed him to the bone.[37]

> Now the dog is drowned I shall see both you and my master just as you are used to be, and with your being as you have been, your friends may very reasonably be satisfied.[38]

Several years later Johnson again employed the phrase in a letter to Thrale:

> The black dog I hope always to resist, and in time to drive, though I am deprived of almost all those that used to help me ... When I rise my breakfast is solitary, the black dog waits to share it, from breakfast to dinner he continues barking, except that Dr Brocklesby for a little keeps him at a distance ... Night comes at last, and some hours of restlessness and confusion bring me again to a day of solitude. What shall exclude the black dog from a habitation like this?[39]

'Black dog' was not simply a code term shared by the pair, for Johnson wrote to his biographer, James Boswell:

> In the place where you now are, there is much to be observed ... But what will you do to keep away the black dog that worries you at home? ... The great direction which Burton has left to men disordered like you, is this, Be not solitary; be not idle: which I would thus modify;– If you are idle, be not solitary; if you are solitary, be not idle.[40]

Johnson recommended that his friend divert himself with investigations of Scottish history. Boswell replied about a fortnight later:

> I now leave Old England in such a state of mind as I am thankful to GOD for granting me. The black dog that worries me at home I cannot but dread; yet as I have been for some time past in a military train, I trust I shall repulse him.[41]

'Black dog' thus appears to have been a familiar expression amongst Johnson and his friends, although Johnson did not include it in his famous dictionary, perhaps not regarding it as 'standard English'.[42] May we, nevertheless, assume that the 'black dog' of melancholy was a Johnsonian creation? We are fortunate in that Mrs Thrale, at the behest of Johnson, maintained a diary, in which we read for the first time the full phrase passed down by Churchill's nanny (19 October 1790):

> The Black Dog is upon his Back; was a common saying some Years ago when a Man was seen troubled with Melancholy: we used to make it a sort of Byword or Hack Joke here at Streatham, and in the Letters I published between Dr Johnson & myself, it is almost

perpetually recurring. Few people however seem to recognize its true Original; which may be found in Dr Henry More's Philosophical Works, where he tells us that Appollonius Tyaneus told the Greeks how that Spirit which was the Scourge of the City where he dwelt, (Athens I think,) appeared to him in Form of a large Black Dog: & leaping on his Back sometimes;– filled him with Melancholy for many Days after.[43]

Apollonius of Tyana (c.3–97 AD) was a neo-Pythagorean philosopher and miracle worker, seen by some as a heathen counterpart to Jesus Christ. Our knowledge concerning him is largely derived from a biography by Philostratus (170–245), but Mrs Thrale encountered the sage indirectly, via the Cambridge theologian–philosopher More; her editor suggested the *Grand Mystery of Godliness* as her source,[44] but she specifically mentions the *Philosophical Works* (which include long discussions of melancholy and its religious significance).[45]

That the intellectually illustrious Streatham circle might adopt 'black dog' from such a source is not implausible, but I have been able to reconcile Mrs Thrale's recollection neither with More nor with Philostratus. What both reported was that Apollonius ended a pestilence in Ephesus by having the towns-people stone to death a demon disguised as an old beggar:

when they … uncovered the heap, [it] appear'd in the shape of an huge black Dog as big as the biggest Lion. This could be no imposture of Melancholy, nor Fraud of any Priest.[46]

There are many shaggy dogs in More's works, but none which haunted Apollonius in the manner remembered by Mrs Thrale. There may be some confusion about cause and effect, for More, like many of his contemporaries, believed 'melancholy' could cause sufferers to see 'phantasms', particularly black dogs.[47] For example, he employed 'black dog' as a metaphor for the 'shadowy Melancholiz'd imagination' when he suggested that 'the black dog may be at the bottome' of certain 'fiery notions and strange Fantasmes' which purport to represent divine revelation.[48] Further, demon possession was often attributed by sceptical minds to melancholy; in one case a woman who had suffered fits for several years:

> fell on the Floor like a Block, and having lain so a while, cryed out, He is gone, he is gone, the Black Dog is gone, and she never had a Fit after.[49]

A recent dictionary, dating 'black dog' to the 1700s, argues that the expression derives from the fact that one 'may be depressed because of the devil's influence'.[50] But the reverse relationship was assumed in the 1700s: if he existed, the Devil could exploit minds already debilitated by melancholy. In any case, 'to have a devil on one's back' had quite a different meaning, and there is no evidence that it was ever used for melancholy, so that its relevance to our 'black dog' is questionable. Johnson's 'black dog' certainly did not appear to involve the Devil, figuratively or otherwise.

In any event, Mrs Thrale later expressed reservations about her first attempt at etymology; having become acquainted with the story of Cardinal Crescence in Burton's *Anatomy*, she suggested that it was probably there that Johnson had discovered the 'black dog' metaphor.[51]

This second explanation is interesting in that Johnson himself suffered from a decidedly oppressive religious melancholia. 'Melancholy' was until recent times more a collective term for a variety of psychological variations, ranging from lethargy to dementia, than a specific complaint;[52] the pioneering brain researcher Thomas Willis defined it as 'madness without fever or frenzy, accompanied by fear and sadness'

(1681).[53] 'Depression' itself was a term not widely used until the twentieth century.

Interestingly, Johnson was one of the first to employ it in the modern sense (though not in his dictionary), describing himself in 1761 as being 'under great depression'.[54]

Excessive melancholy was long regarded as sinful disregard for God's gracious arrangement of the world (*acedia*),[55] but 'hypochondria' or 'melancholy' had been 'fashionable' in England since Shakespeare's time:

> These pleasures, Melancholy, give
> And I with thee will choose to live. [56]

Unlike many intellectuals and artists of his time, however, Johnson did not regard melancholy as the stylish accompaniment of genius, but rather as an intolerable burden which perhaps presaged the total loss of both his intellectual function and his salvation, and which he attributed to perceived personal failings not entirely apparent to others. Johnson's 'black dog' was thus an expression not only of his abject misery, but also of his guilt and fear of damnation. As such, Johnson's complex pain is more familiar to sufferers of clinical depression than the languid melancholia of some of his contemporaries.

Outside the Johnson circle, there is little indication that the 'black dog' was widely invoked, a curious exception being its inclusion by Johnson's friend and fellow Streathamite, Giuseppe Baretti (1719–1789), in his English–Italian dictionary (1790):

> To have the black dog, *essere di cattivissimo umore, essere molto maninconoso* [to be in terrible humor, to be very melancholic] [57]

Nor did the phrase appear in contemporary dictionaries of conventional or unconventional English, although the similar 'to walk the black dog on someone' was recorded late in the eighteenth century:

> a punishment inflicted in the night on a fresh prisoner, by his comrades, in case of his refusal to pay the usual footing or garnish.[58]

'Black dog' was employed only infrequently in literature. Walter Scott used 'black dog' for 'ill humour' in the early nineteenth century:

> I think [the angry] Sir Arthur has got the black dog on his back again', said Miss Oldbuck. 'Black dog! – Black devil! He's more absurd than womankind.' (1816)[59]

> I passed a pleasant day with kind J.B., which was a great relief from the black dog, which would have worried me at home. (1826)[60]

Somewhat later, Robert Louis Stevenson described Montigny, a 'gamester', in the *New Arabian Nights* (1882):

> He did not seem to be enjoying his luck. His mouth was a little to a side; one nostril nearly shut, and the other much inflated. The black dog was on his back, as people say, in terrifying nursery metaphor; and he breathed hard under the gruesome burden.[61]

In his exhaustive compilation of 'canine terms applied to human beings',[62] the American English professor, Tom Burns Haber, interpreted 'black dog' here as 'nervous fit', but was correctly criticised by a colleague who suggested that the context suggested 'ill humour'.[63] Secondly, the sea-captain is approached at the beginning of Stevenson's *Treasure Island* (1883) by a stranger whom he immediately recognises with alarm as an old acquaintance, Black Dog. An altercation ensues; the captain collapses, but eventually recovers:

... suddenly his colour changed, and he tried to raise himself, crying, 'Where's Black Dog?' 'There is no Black Dog here,' said the doctor, 'except what you have on your own back. You have been drinking rum; you have had a stroke, precisely as I told you; and I have just, very much against my own will, dragged you headforemost out of the grave.' [64]

'Black dog': An English problem?

It is notable that references to the 'black dog' are most common in England. One of the few American references stems from James Branch Cabell in his satanic novel *Jurgen* (1919):

So come now, make yourself fine, and shake the black dog from your back, for we are spending the evening with the Asmodeuses. [65]

Nor do American discussions of metaphors for depression include 'black dog'. [66] Abraham Lincoln is occasionally said to have referred to his depression as his 'black dog', but a precise source is never given. [67] Nor is 'black dog' generally employed for depression in non-English speaking countries without reference to its Churchillian origins, although a German reviewer could comment (on a typically melancholic Finnish film, *Juha*):

a black dog is also again to be seen, now and then, emblem of the melancholic. [68]

There is no shortage of European references to 'black dogs' (many guarding treasures, or signifying, for example, damnation in Brittany), [69] or evil canines (the Grimms' 'big bad wolf'), nor of canine linguistic allusions (especially in German), but no reference to our 'black dog'. Maybe the English predilection for depression simply demanded a larger descriptive vocabulary, as suggested by the prominent Parisian physician Philippe Pinel:

One should perhaps admire the unfortunate fertility of the English for vigorous, apposite expressions for the extreme perplexity, depression and despair of the melancholic, even in their medical works, not to mention their novels and poetry.[70]

Neither this nor Montesquieu's (1689–1755) assertion that the English tended to commit suicide without apparent reason [71] was purely French invective; the English themselves were of similar opinion:

> Melancholy is a kind of Demon that haunts our Island ...[72]

> The Title I have chosen for this treatise, is a Reproach universally thrown on this island by Foreigners and all our Neighbours on the Continent, by whom nervous Distempers, Spleen, Vapours, and lowness of Spirits, are in derision, called the ENGLISH MALADY. And I wish there were not so good Grounds for this Reflection ...[73]

The author of the last lines, George Cheyne, was physician to Samuel Johnson, and advanced many plausible reasons for the prevalence of melancholy in England – the land itself, the climate, the food, the dissolute lifestyle.

Something else peculiar to the British Isles is the prominence of legends concerning black dogs, such as the Dartmoor Black Dog, adapted by Conan Doyle for his *Hound of the Baskervilles* (1902). Similar stories are also reported in America, but are not as widespread. The British Isles, in comparison, are infested with ghostly hounds, many dating back to traditions and practices of Celtic times: from the Barguest of Yorkshire to the Mauthe Dog of Man, from the Sliab Mis hound in Kerry to the Whist Hounds of Devon – monstrous black dogs, alone or in packs, seen at night or, with luck, only heard while passing, shaggy and with eyes that glow like coals, render the countryside unsafe. Some house unquiet souls, others the Devil himself.[74]

With these legends firmly embedded in British consciousness, it is not surprising that, in some areas, the dark hound is emblematic for disquiet of one's own soul:

> In my Scots–Irish family, dealing with depression is called 'wrestling with the black dog'. I thought it was peculiar to us – both the experience and the phrase for it – but then in my early thirties I read a biography of the nineteenth century Anglo-Irish explorer Sir Richard Burton [1821–1890] ... after a great achievement (like translating *1001 Nights* or being the first non-Muslim to penetrate Mecca) Burton would feel a loss of purpose and fall into deep depressions that could last for months on end, periods where he would say he was 'wrestling with the black dog' ... [In] a number of Irish folk tales, the devil appears in the form of a black beast or hound that runs alongside a traveler at night, with glowing red eyes and an air of implacable menace. Sometimes the dog must be wrestled, and beaten, if the traveler is to survive. It struck me that these tales must be pre-Christian, and that we all have our devils running alongside of us.[75]

As mentioned above, Chambers had implied in 1864 that the expression 'black dog on the back' was related to British 'spectre-dogs', but did not further elaborate.[76] A connection between the ghostly hounds and the 'black dog' of melancholy would appear, however, more than plausible.

'Black dog' in the twentieth century

'Black dog' began to appear in dictionaries at the end of the nineteenth century, as discussed above, but in the early twentieth century it was defined primarily as 'delirium tremens',[77] a meaning it had carried since the mid-nineteenth century.[78] Interestingly, American expressions for melancholy and delirium tremens overlapped to some extent, including, for example, the use of 'blue devils' and 'jim jams' for both, but here 'black dog' referred only to delirium tremens.[79]

As suggested by Colville in his comments on Churchill, it seems that 'black dog' survived into the twentieth century within certain families, even where they were unaware of its use outside their own circle. It was never widely employed in published material, seeming instead to be part of the spoken vernacular. A number of (mostly British crime) writers used 'black dog on the back' from the 1930s onwards for 'bad mood' or 'annoyance' ('If I don't talk to somebody soon … I shall get a black dog on my back').[80] Robert Mitchum remarked to Teresa Wright in the western *Pursued* (1941) that their lives had been marked by 'a black dog riding my back and yours too', but this appears to be more akin to 'devil on the back' than our black dog.

It is ultimately unlikely that 'black dog' was a specific term for depression before Churchill used it, but was rather a vague reference to anything which rendered someone less than congenial, whether ill temper, fear, guilt or, indeed, melancholy; as recently as 1956, it was defined simply as 'peevish fit', especially in children.[81] Other terms which also began their ascent in the eighteenth century – the 'blue devils' (1780s), 'the blues' (1740s) [82] and more general descriptions of depressed spirits – were more frequently recorded, at least in published texts, and generally retained a more specific relationship with 'depression'. Adoption of 'black dog' by Churchill (and by those who write about him) thus represented a turning point for the beast; and once the adoption became public, whatever it was exactly that Churchill meant, 'black dog' could assume its now secure place in English as a metaphor for depression.[83]

But how secure? Eric Partridge (1894–1979), well respected for his books on language, and particularly interested in historical slang, wrote (1961):

> black dog (sitting) on one's back, have (got) a. To be
> depressed: coll[oquial]: late C.19–20; ob[solescent] [84]

He thus regarded 'black dog' as being of quite recent origin, but also almost obsolete – none of which concurs with what we have discussed. Interestingly, he also mentioned an expression which I have not otherwise encountered:

> Pompey (or the black dog Pompey) is on your back! a
> c[atch]-p[hrase] (–1869) addressed to a fractious child:
> provincial coll[oquial], and dial[ectic].[85]

Regardless: since Churchill inadvertently popularised the term, 'black dog' has not only been adopted by sufferers of depression and their physicians, but also by literary [86] and musical circles.[87] It is also interesting that, despite the century-old *OED* definition of 'black dog' cited above, the *Concise OED* defined it until 1971 only as 'sulks'; the sixth edition added the less negative 'melancholy mood', perhaps reflecting a changed attitude towards the nature of depression.

And why is 'black dog' ultimately such a popular term? Perhaps because it reflects a certain attitude to the experience of depression: it externalises the dark feelings as a companion, albeit an unwelcome companion; it expresses some of the oppression not heard in 'depression' (in contrast, for example, to the German *Niedergeschlagenheit* and *Gedrücktheit*); it emphasises, in contrast to earlier romantic–intellectual interpretations of melancholia, that depression may be distinct from the underlying personality. In this sense, it is a metaphor of hope: the 'black dog' may be to some extent a friend, but he is a bad friend; and as with anyone who renders life miserable and restricts interactions and possibilities, he needs to be left behind, no matter how persistent his pursuit.

Come over here black dog
and I'll pat you on your head
you've been following me for a good long time
I guess you must be my friend
I guess you must be my good friend

I don't want you to be my friend no more black dog:
I don't want you to come around.[88]

SECOND PRIZE

BLACK BILE AND MAN'S BEST FRIEND:
A history of the Black Dog

DAVID MUSGRAVE

Last Christmas while visiting my parents-in-law's farm on the western plains of New South Wales, I was bitten by Oscar, one of my father-in-law's dogs. It was a cheeky little nip on the ankle that failed to draw blood and earned him a smack and a scolding, but didn't stop him from repeating the offence a number of times over the week we were there. Quite some time later I discovered that Oscar did not belong to the family of dogs born and bred on the farm, all named by my father-in-law after his mother-in law's brothers and sisters (Oscar was the exception: it was the name of my father-in-law's father-in-law, my wife's grandfather). He had been sent to them through the agency of a friend in Sydney because of a number of behavioural problems which made it impossible for his Sydney owners to keep him. One of those misdemeanours was to bite the visiting former US president Bill Clinton one morning as he took an early morning stroll somewhere in Rushcutters Bay. Naturally, my first reaction on learning this was immense pride, knowing that I had been bitten by the same dog that had bitten an American president. For a while, my boasting knew no bounds: apart from being a pair of charismatic devils, Bill Clinton and I had something else in common.

It wasn't long, however, before I returned to Sydney to the job which, while being merely adequate to the mortgage which we had taken out the year before, had its own array of cares, frustrations and political games. In fact, it wasn't long before I had slipped into a kind of malaise, less intense than those which I had experienced in my twenties, but nonetheless pervasive, one which constrained the horizon of what I believed to be possible, leaving me with a sensation of being trapped, unable to do anything or go anywhere that might make a difference or relieve the suffering. Whatever it was that had taken hold of me dogged me wherever I went and showed no sign of letting go. In fact, I told a number of my friends that I was being visited by the black dog every day and couldn't see my way clear to be rid of him. A number of weeks passed and gradually I shook off that episode of depression. I threw myself back into my work, found pleasure once more in my studies and resumed the writing projects which I had not been able to face for some time.

One of those projects turned out, eventually, to be this essay. I had a personal interest in the history of the 'black dog', and the opportunity to write about it and account for how this expression came into currency in English was a challenge I relished. To my mind, the crucial questions to be asked about the history of the black dog are these: why a dog? and why black and not some other colour? It struck me, however, before I delved into an exhaustive search of the literature that there was more to be learned from considering that episode with Oscar and my illustrious co-bitee than any history of the occurrence of that phrase in English literature.

Oscar is not a black dog (he is a floppy-eared, piebald Jack Russell), but his misbehaviour embodied the deep ambivalence that the dog possesses in our culture. The dog is a companion, man's best friend as the cliché goes. As an object of affectional touch and hugging, the dog serves basic human emotional needs.[1] But, paradoxically, the dog is valuable to us because it retains many of the characteristics of the wolf from which it is descended: a distrust of strangers and a marked territorialism (making it an ideal guardian of self and property); the ability to herd and hunt. Yet, for all that, a dog can bite (and does). The deep familiarity of the dog to the human sits alongside that part of its nature which is unfamiliar and alien, and it is the uneasy co-existence of these qualities that is the genesis for the term 'black dog'. Then there is the blackness of the black dog, which points back to a folkloric tradition and, beyond that, to an ancient philosophical theory of the humours. But before delving into that history, it is worthwhile trying to pin-point the moment when the term 'black dog' entered into English as a specific description of depression: this has as much to do with the evolution of the term 'depression', in distinction from the earlier, more encompassing term 'melancholy', as it does with a sudden shift of the usage of 'black dog' as a figure of folklore to a figure of personalised, psychological description.

It is mistakenly assumed that Horace was the first to make reference to the 'black dog' of depression. There are plenty of dogs in Horace's odes, epodes, epistles and satires, but nowhere are they described as black. In the twenty-seventh ode of the third book, Horace writes of several evil omens, among them

> ... *praegnas canis au tab agro*
> *rava decurrens lupa Lanuvino*
> *fetaque vulpes,*

which James Michie translates as

> ... a pregnant bitch, a vixen
> Swollen with cubs, or a grey she-wolf lolloping
> Down from Lavinium.[2]

There is certainly a strong tradition emanating from this,

which later includes the black dog as a sign of bad luck or as a sign of the Devil, as in Goethe's *Faust*, where Mephistopheles first appears to Faust in the form of a black dog,[3] and as mentioned by that seventeenth-century scholar and anatomiser of melancholy, Robert Burton, who writes of a superstitious person that 'every black dog or cat he sees he suspecteth to be a Devil'.[4] But these instances are more than a millennium apart, and a vast tradition of pagan as well as Christian folklore intervenes.

Elsewhere Horace writes of *atra cura*, or 'black care', and it is this recurrent phrase which has been mistranslated as 'black dog', most notably by the Victorian scholar Sir John Conington who, in 1869, translated this passage from the seventh satire of the second book:

> *adde, quod idem*
> *non horam tecum esse potes, non otia recte*
> *ponere, teque ipsum vitas fugitives et erro*
> *iam vino quaerens, iam somno fallere Curam;*
> *frustra: nam comes atra premit sequiturque fugacem.*[5]

as

> Then too you cannot spend an hour alone;
> No company's more hateful than your own;
> You dodge and give yourself the slip; you seek
> In bed or in your cups from care to sneak:
> In vain: the black dog follows you, and hangs
> Close on your flying skirts with hungry fangs[6]

when in actual fact a more accurate translation is something like Fairclough's:

> And again, you cannot yourself bear to be in your own company, you cannot employ your leisure aright, you shun yourself, a runaway and vagabond, seeking now

with wine, and now with sleep, to baffle Care. In vain:
that black consort dogs and follows your flight.[7]

Not a canine fang in sight! It is possible to sympathise with Conington's imaginative depiction of black care as a black dog simply because the expression is now, and was before Conington translated, in common parlance (not to mention the rhyme of 'hangs' with 'fangs'). But there is nothing in Horace to suggest a 'black dog' either here or elsewhere where 'black care' appears. In the first ode of the third book, Horace writes

post equitem sedet atra Cura

which is translated by Michie as

behind the horseman squats black care[8]

and which, if it was not for the malignant connotations of the word 'squat', could well be a description of a dog, much like one of my father-in-law's, perched on the back of his speeding motorcycle, tongue lolling joyfully in the breeze. By the time we trawl through all of Horace and read, in the eleventh ode of the fourth book, that he recommends a good song as a remedy for the 'ravages inflicted by black care',[9] it is clear that his 'black care' has much in common with our 'black dog'. The real question is, why is it black?

Aristotle was among the first of the ancients to divide everything into four constituent elements: fire, earth, air and water, which were formed by combination of the four primary qualities of matter: cold, heat, wetness and dryness.[10] In turn, Hippocrates theorised that the human temperament and physique were determined by the presence in the body of four humours which corresponded to the four elements. These were:

- sanguine – blood (air; moist and hot)
- melancholic – black bile (earth; dry and cold)

- choleric – yellow bile (fire; dry and hot)
- phlegmatic – phlegm (water; moist and cold).[11]

The influence of this 'humoral' pathology has persisted through the Middle Ages to this day, with its heyday being in the sixteenth and seventeenth centuries. 'Sanguine' and 'phlegmatic' are still common descriptions of character, and 'melancholy' is a common adjective (even if markedly different from its meaning in the seventeenth century) used to denote sadness. The word 'melancholy' originally, and unequivocally, meant madness, but included within its broad ambit anxiety, sadness and delusion. Timothy Bright's *A Treatise of Melancholie* (1586) illustrates nicely the supposed relationship between the pathological condition of melancholy and its physical, humoral basis:

> The perturbations of melancholy are for the most parte, sadde and fearful, and such as rise of them: as distrust, doubt, diffidence, or dispaire, sometimes furious and sometimes merry in apparaunce, through a kinde of Sardonian, and false laughter, as the humour is disposed that procureth these diversities. Those which are sad and pensive, rise of that melancholick humour, which is the grossest part of the blood, whether it be iuice or excrement, not passing the naturall temper in heat whereof it partaketh, and is called cold in comparison onely. This for the most part is setled in the spleane, and with his vapours anoyeth the harte and passing vp to the brayne, counterfetteth terrible obiectes to the fantasie, and polluting both the substance, and spirits of the brayne, causeth it without externall occasion, to forge monstrous fictions, and terrible to the conceite, which the iudgement taking as they are presented by the disordered instrument, deliuer ouer to the hart, which hath no

iudgement of discretion in it self, but giuing credite to the mistaken report of the braine, breaketh out into that inordinate passion, against reason.[12]

By far the most comprehensive resource we have regarding late Renaissance thinking about melancholy is Robert Burton's massive *Anatomy of Melancholy*, which first appeared in 1621 and which he continued working on until his death in 1640. Burton was a scholar who lived all his life at Oxford; it is said that for amusement he would wander down each day to the canals where he would laugh at the profanities and swearing of the boatmen. The *Anatomy* is a work of genius which combines medical knowledge with enormous erudition, humour, poetry and fantasy. Its treatment of the theme of melancholy is more than encyclopaedic: its Byzantine partitions, sections, members and subsections deal variously with the causes of melancholy and its cures, of love-melancholy and of myriad digressions from an overwhelming number of sources (including Horace). It is clear from the *Anatomy* that melancholy is a broad category of madness, unreason as well as what we would term depression. There is no reference in it to any 'black dog' specifically associated with, or embodying, depression or melancholy. Rather, black dogs appear in a superstitious sense, as noted above, or in a supernatural sense as when Burton, citing the authority of the sixteenth-century Italian polymath Girolamo Cardano, notes of terrestrial devils that

> they sometimes appear in the likeness of hares, crows, black dogs.[13]

The *Anatomy of Melancholy* remained one of the most popular and widely read books for succeeding centuries, appearing in 40 editions, and it was the favourite reading of Samuel Johnson, of whom Boswell remarks:

Burton's *Anatomy of Melancholy*, he said, was the only book that ever took him out of bed two hours sooner than he wished to rise.[14]

Doctor Johnson is also the first person in English who is recorded as having referred to the black dog as an embodiment of psychological depression.

It therefore makes sense that the term 'black dog', used as a description or name for depression, came into usage some time between 1640 and 1779. In a letter to Mrs Thrale, Johnson remarked that:

> The Black Dog I hope always to resist, and in time to drive, though I am deprived of almost all those that used to help me... When I rise my breakfast is solitary, the Black Dog waits to share it, from breakfast to dinner he continues barking, except that Dr. Brocklesby for a little keeps him at a distance... Night comes at last, and some hours of restlessness and confusion bring me again to a day of solitude. What shall exclude the Black Dog from a habitation like this?

And then goes on to speculate wistfully on an ideal solution to his predicament:

> If I were a little richer, I would perhaps take some cheerful female into the house. [15]

The black dog is mentioned in several letters between Doctor Johnson and Mrs Thrale. For example, the first reference occurs in a letter concerning Mrs Thrale's husband:

> To Mrs Thrale
> October 31, 1778
>
> Dear Madam,
> Your letter seemed very long a-coming, and was very welcome at last; do not be so long again.

> Long live Sir John Shelly, that lures my master to hunt. I hope he will soon shake off the black dog, and come here as light as a feather.[16]

To which Mrs Thrale replies from Brighton:

> My Master swims now and forgets the black dog.[17]

Johnson's reply in turn continues the metaphor:

> I shall easily forgive my master his long stay, if he leaves the dog behind him. We will watch, as well as we can, that the dog shall never be let in again, for when he comes the first thing he does is to worry my master.[18]

And then continues in a vein which suggests that the 'black dog', which seems to have afflicted Mr Thrale, has now been transferred to Johnson:

> a vile one it is, but I hope if he is not hanged he is drowned; with another lusty shake he will pick my master's heart out.
>
> I have begun to take valerian.[19]

And then triumphantly declares some weeks later:

> Now the dog is drowned.[20]

The phrase was not merely part of a private language between Mrs Thrale and Johnson; Johnson writes to Boswell with equal familiarity (and concern):

> But what will you do to keep away the *black dog* that worries you at home?[21]

It is Hester Thrale, however, who provides us with the greatest clues as to the origin of the black dog which peppers her correspondence with Doctor Johnson. In her diary, she writes:

> The *Black Dog* is upon his back, was a common

expression some Years ago when a Man was seen troubled with Melancholy: we used to make of it a sort of *Byword* or *Hack Joke* here at Steatham, and in the letters I published between Dr Johnson & myself, it is almost perpetually recurring.

Few People however seem to recognize its true Original; which may be found in Dr Henry More's Philosophical Works, where he tells us that Appollonius [sic.] Tyaneus told the Greeks how that Spirit which was the Scourge of the City where he dwelt, (Athens I think) appeared to him in Form of a large *Black Dog: & leaping on his Back* sometimes; – filled him with Melancholy for many Days after.[22]

Henry More was a philosopher and one of the Cambridge Platonists who was drawn to mysticism and theosophy in later life. His *Opera Philosophica* appeared in 1678, some 38 years after Burton's death. The anecdote concerning Apollonius does not appear in Burton's *Anatomy* (although there are at least a dozen instances where he does) and most likely came from Philostratus' *Life of Apollonius*, with which More was obviously familiar, as it would have been his source. But this is of little import: with the same ease with which she wrote, Mrs Thrale later changes her mind regarding the origin of the saying:

I have mentioned the *Black Dog* as of Greek Original in this Analect Book sometime; but one may find it nearer home it seems: Cardinal Crescenza at Verona died mad, he had for many Years fancied himself pursued by a *Black Dog* & complained during his last Hours that nobody would keep that beast off his Bed. The Story is quoted in Burton's *Anatomy of Melancholy*, where I dare say Doctor Johnson read it.

And then sniffs somewhat disapprovingly:

That Book has been exceedingly pillaged.[23]

We know that Johnson was besotted with Burton's *Anatomy*, as were many of his contemporaries, including Laurence Sterne, and even those of the Romantic era such as Keats and Byron. It is reasonable to suppose that Johnson, who was essentially endowed with a scholarly and critical faculty as well as being a poet, would have brought into parlance a metaphor he picked up from his reading. The other point worth making is this: Johnson chose to use a phrase that derived from popular expression, influenced by his knowledge of, and deep reading in, the subject of melancholy. Why did he not refer to his bouts of 'black dog' as melancholia? Because by the time Johnson was writing, melancholy had ceased to be an important concept of pathology and psychology and had become instead a widely used adjective to describe sadness – and anyone who has experienced depression will know that neither 'depression' nor 'melancholy' is adequate to describe what William Styron calls 'a howling tempest in the brain.'[24]

Nonetheless, it is Johnson's correspondent Mrs Thrale who provides us with evidence that the original phrase which anteceded hers and Johnson's use of it was 'the *Black Dog* is upon his back', used to describe someone afflicted by melancholy. And from where did that phrase originate? From the mass popularity of Henry More's philosophical works? Or from the common knowledge of Burton's *Anatomy*? Unlikely. In a footnote to Mrs Thrales' second derivation of the term, her editor, Katharine Balderstone, remarks:

The black dog is, however a common folk superstition. See Chambers's *Book of Days*, ii. 433.[25]

And Balderstone is indeed correct, although not nearly so much as she thinks. Robert Chambers' *Book of Days* was an exceedingly popular miscellany of significant dates, folkloric superstition and 'popular antiquities', published in 1879. In the section relating to spectre-dogs (October 11 – now a day I will forever remember as 'black dog day'), Chambers writes that

> spectre-dogs … occupy a distinct branch of English mythology [and] are supposed to exist in one form or another in almost every county.[26]

He goes on:

> To have the 'black dog on the back' has become a general phrase, though perhaps few who use it have an idea of its origin. The following anecdotes about spectre-dogs will illustrate this phrase, and shew how generally this branch of superstition is received.[27]

But the illustrations which Chambers provides do not convincingly make the link between the black dog as a spectral presence and the term 'black dog' as a term relating to depression. The black dog apparition, which is one of three kinds of spectre-dog (the others being spirits or evil persons who have been transformed into dogs as punishment and evil spirits which assume the form and habits of hounds), has the same general characteristics wherever it appears:

> It is described as large, shaggy, and black, with long ears and tail. It does not belong to any species of living dogs, but is severally said to resemble a hound, a setter, a terrier, or a shepherd-dog, though often larger than a Newfoundland. It bears different names, but is always alike supposed to be an evil spirit, haunting places where evil deeds have been done, or where some calamity may be expected.[28]

From there on several anecdotes are enumerated, one of which Chambers claims to have witnessed himself, two others of which were related to him by eyewitnesses and all of which relate to the supernatural. Some of these are well known: the Lyme Regis and Bungay black dogs, among others. Chambers distances himself from the veracity of all these manifestations (presumably including his own) by concluding that

> it has been fully and satisfactorily ascertained that the goblin-hounds, which have originated such fanciful legends in almost every county, are merely flocks of wild-geese, or other large migratory birds.[29]

Obviously, the implication is that a spectral manifestation presaging misfortune or calamity, however doubtful in its authenticity, is the origin of a phrase which over one hundred years prior to his writing had come to mean a state of melancholy or depression. The inference is not without basis: in his anecdotes, the presence of a black dog induces anxiety, dread and so on in its victims, each of which belongs to a general state of depression.

However, this explanation does not fully account for the use to which the phrase was put by Johnson and, following him, Sir John Conington in his translations of Horace, Sir Richard Burton in his translations of *The Arabian Nights* and in his letters, and, most famously of all, Sir Winston Churchill. A brief consideration of the history of the metaphor in the hands of these famous exemplars tells us a lot about how it has developed over time, as well as from where it can be truly said to have originated. For example, the terms which qualify Johnson's metaphor: his black dog barks continuously from breakfast to dinner, it has teeth, it weighs on its victim and must be shaken off, threatening to tear out his heart – all of which agrees with the spectral tradition of the black dog. But it is also a curiously intimate manifestation: it waits to share Johnson's otherwise solitary breakfast, Doctor Brocklesby keeps it at a distance for a while and Johnson's main anxiety is that it be *let in* – all of which is in distinction to the black dog which typically appears at night on the road, in the hedgerow or in the ditch. There is much of the black bile in these metaphors, an anxiety which has internalised the spectral apparition of folklore and imbued it with the peculiar intensity of melancholy.

It follows that subsequent references to the 'black dog' retain traces of this fusion of the scholarly tradition of melancholy with the folkloric tradition of the spectral dog – Conington's translation of Horace is all fangs and dogged pursuit, but insubstantial nonetheless, and directly related to care or worry. The explorer and linguist Sir Richard Burton was said to have wrestled with the black dog after a great achievement, but this characterisation of depression has lost all physicality, despite the wrestling metaphor, and is merely akin to an abstract struggle, as with one's conscience. The most famous example of all, Winston Churchill's reference to his 'fits of depression that might last for months [as] the "Black Dog"'[30], represents the furthest remove from the expression's folkloric and melancholic/humoral origins: the black dog has become sufficient in itself as a synonym for depression, but remains in use because it is a powerfully personal description of an otherwise 'clinical' disorder, and still retains traces of its humanistic and folkloric origins.

While I have been successful in eluding or avoiding my black dog for some time now, I was interested to learn, after reading about Bill Clinton's quadruple bypass, that depression is one common side-effect of open heart surgery.[31] Although he is someone who seems never to have been subject to bouts of depression before, it would be interesting to know if, sitting up in his hospital bed, chatting with Hillary about how he was going to give up fried chicken and hamburgers for lentil-burgers and skinless, boiled chicken (and feeling, as he speaks, a small, unfamiliar pit of depression forming in his stomach), whether he caught a fleeting glimpse out of the corner of his eye of something that reminded him of that piebald, rascally pup that nipped him on the ankle in Australia two years before; only this would be a much darker beast, black as melancholy and perpetually on the periphery of his vision, much harder to pin down than any ordinary dog, yet somehow always there. It's possible. But I can't imagine Bill Clinton's black dog lasting for very long, can you?

Bibliography

Aristotle, *The Physics*, vol. 1 (tran. Philip H Wicksteed & Francis M Cornford, 1929) William Heinemann, London.

Boswell, James, *The Life of Samuel Johnson*, vol. 2 (ed. George Birkbeck Hill, revised LF Powell, 1934) Clarendon Press, Oxford.

Bright, Timothy, 1940 (1586), *A Treatise of Melancholie*, Facsimile Text Society, New York.

Burton, Robert, *The Anatomy of Melancholy* (ed. Floyd Dell & Paul Jordan-Smith, 1927) Tudor, New York.

Chambers, Robert, 1879, *Book of Days: A Miscellany of Popular Antiquities in Connection with the Calendar*, vol 2, JB Lippincott, Philadelphia.

Goethe, Johann Wolfgang von, *Faust* (tran. John Anster, 1985) Harrap, London.

Hippocrates, *The Genuine Works of Hippocrates*, vol. 1 (tran. Francis Adams, 1849) The Sydenham Society, London.

Horace, *The Odes of Horace* (tran. James Michie, 1970) Penguin, Harmondsworth.

Horace, *Satires, Epistles and Ars Poetica* (trans. H Rushton Fairclough, 1999) Harvard University Press, Cambridge MA.

Horace, *The Satires, Epistles and Art of Poetry of Horace* (trans. John Conington, 1902) George Bell, London.

Johnson, Samuel, *Letters of Samuel Johnson*, vol. 2, Jan. 15, 1777–Dec. 18, 1784 (ed. George Birkbeck Hill, 1892) Clarendon, Oxford.

Meyer, W & Pakur, M, 1999, 'Thoughts about the domestic dog as the catalyst for relations between humans and a body contact object for humans', *Schweiz Arch Tierheilkd*, 141(8), pp. 351–9.

Moran, Lord, 1966, *Winston Churchill: The Struggle for Survival 1940–1965*, Constable, London.

Thrale, Hester, *Thraliana: The Diary of Mrs Hester Lynch Thrale (later Mrs Piozzi) 1776–1809*, vol. 2 1784–1809 (ed. Katharine C Balderston, 1942) Clarendon, Oxford.

THIRD PRIZE

CHURCHILL'S BLACK DOG?
The history of the Black Dog as a metaphor for depression

MEGAN McKINLAY

The dog and man have a long and complex history of interaction, full of ambivalent and contradictory significations. Both classical and contemporary iconography and symbology – as represented in art, literature, popular culture and the images of ancient mythologies – feature a myriad of canine incarnations, figures whose presence resonates with a significance beyond the contours of their physical form. In the competing and complementary representations of classical mythology, dogs menace, defile, and patrol borders, both earthly and supernatural, but also heal, protect, purify, and act as symbols of loyalty and fidelity. In modern parlance, we let sleeping dogs lie; we go to the dogs or die like a dog; we dog someone at every turn, or compete in a dog-eat-dog environment. And when we put a name to our depression, increasingly it is that of the black dog, lurking behind us, or clinging tenaciously to our backs. The statesman and politician Winston Churchill drew upon this image to conceptualise his own struggle with depression, and it is with him that the metaphor is generally associated. Indeed, so firmly linked are the man and the image in contemporary usage that some references make the man an integral part of the metaphor. When an Australian band sang about fighting depression, they talked of making peace with 'Churchill's Black

Dog', and the phrase became the title for a popular song.[1] In a similar process, The Black Dog Institute of Australia takes as its logo Churchill's famous 'V for victory' sign casting a shadow in the form of a black dog. Contemporary representations such as these both reflect and perpetuate the popular belief in Churchill as the originator of the phrase, solidifying the association in the minds of the public.

In a strictly historical sense, this understanding of the phrase is clearly misleading. The black dog is not Churchill's, at least not originally. That he referred to his own depression in these terms is indisputable. However, also indisputable is the fact that Hester Thrale, Samuel Johnson, and James Boswell all used the phrase to refer to a similar state in their prolific eighteenth-century correspondence. To this readily accessible textual evidence, we might add the fact that the menacing connotations of the black dog had been established well before this point, via the folklore of Britain and Europe, the influence of Greek and Roman mythologies, and a growing body of literature in which black dogs featured as harbingers of death, or emissaries of the Devil. The popular contemporary association of the black dog with Winston Churchill obscures a complex process of evolution whose investigation brings together not only the classical and the contemporary, but also the fields of mythology, literature, symbology and psychology.

Because of the nature of this evolutionary process, the language historian who embarks on a kind of join-the-dots quest for the definitive origins of a term is likely to be thwarted. Tracing and describing the development of images and symbols, those aspects of language which tap into the creative complexities of the human psyche, is an endeavour far less certain than the simple pursuit of a trail of historical breadcrumbs. Inevitably, there are gaps between one signpost and the next, points at which the historian is obliged to make a leap of assumption, weaving together apparent connections to somehow arrive at a conclusion which arranges these unruly breadcrumbs in a satisfyingly tidy order. To explore the evolution of what has become Churchill's Black Dog is to attempt to cross some of these gaps, remaining mindful of the leaps, the absences, the in-many-cases sheer impossibility of making definitive claims. To track the Black Dog from a modern vantage point requires a movement increasingly away from certainty, from readily available documentation, and into the areas of myth, folklore, and speculation.

For the purposes of this investigation, to begin with the contemporary and move backwards chronologically is to begin with the figure of Churchill himself, the touchstone to whom modern usage of the phrase is inevitably linked. Notwithstanding popular belief, authoritative reference works such as the *Oxford English Dictionary* and *Brewer's Dictionary of Phrase and Fable* make it clear that the metaphor pre-dates Churchill. The *OED* points us towards a generic popular usage, indicating that the phrase 'the black dog is on his back' is used of sulky children in some rural areas,[2] but stops short of providing further details or speculating as to the origin of the usage. The first of the two literary references it cites quotes a passage from Robert Louis Stevenson's *New Arabian Nights* in which a morose character is described as having 'the black dog upon his back'.[3] Interestingly, this 1882 passage suggests that the phrase is already in relatively common usage by this point, claiming that it is drawn from 'terrifying nursery metaphor',[4] perhaps referring to the aforementioned popular usage.

The second of the two literary references cited here is intriguing for another reason. The reference to 'the black dog which would have worried me at home', from Sir Walter Scott's diary entry for May 12, 1826,[5] is an almost verbatim quote of a phrase used by Samuel Johnson in correspondence to James

Boswell in 1779, almost half a century earlier. Johnson writes, in response to a letter from Boswell which has not been traced by historians:

> ... what will you do to keep away the *black dog* that worries you at home?[6]

We will turn our attention to Johnson and his correspondents shortly; the point to note here is not only Scott's almost whole-sale adoption of Johnson's phrase, suggesting an inter-textual process at work in the evolution of the metaphor, but also the failure of the *OED* to identify this earlier and well-documented usage. Turning to Brewer, we see the phrase in a different form, and with no specific reference to children:

> *A black dog has walked over him.* Said of a sullen person. Horace tells us that the sight of a black dog with its pups was an unlucky omen.[7]

Brewer's shortcomings are not those of the *OED*. The entry at least recognises that the Black Dog predates Scott and Stevenson; however, the wholesale leap from the contemporary phrase to the Horace reference seems rather gratuitous. In the first place, there is no direct connection between the two, other than the fact that they both contain references to black dogs. To be sullen or depressed is not at all the same as being 'unlucky', and at any rate, the Horace citation insists on the presence of pups, shifting the emphasis away from the figure of the black dog itself.

Moreover, while it may be tempting to claim the Brewer citation as at least having located the earliest instance of the usage, this is not necessarily the case either. Earlier black-dog references from the Greek classics, which might as readily be linked to the contemporary form of the phrase, predate Horace by several centuries. Plutarch, for example, writes that in around

450 BC, some 400 years earlier, a black dog appeared to the prominent Athenian, Cimon, to announce his impending death.[8] Earlier incarnations of the figure of the black dog in classical mythology will be discussed in more detail as we continue our historical backtracking; for now, the point is that while these canonical reference works are less than reliable on the subject, their authoritative tone has the effect of shutting down further enquiry. Assessments which are essentially partial and subjective naturalise their own version of history in much the same way that contemporary linkage of the phrase with Churchill does. We can no more accept at face value the pronouncements of these references than we can accept the popular belief that Churchill is the originator of the phrase.

A notable omission in both of these citations is the aforementioned Johnson, Boswell, and Thrale. Almost a century before Churchill's birth, these three correspondents were using the phrase amongst themselves to represent a persistent state of melancholy. Among the published letters, the earliest use is found in October, 1778, in a missive from Johnson to Mrs Thrale, where the former writes in reference to the low spirits of her husband, Henry Thrale, referred to by both of them as 'the master':

> I hope he will soon shake off the black dog and come home as light as a feather.[9]

Despite earlier correspondence between both Johnson and Thrale and Johnson and Boswell being liberally peppered with references to melancholy and ill health, both direct and metaphorical – phrases such as 'black fumes', 'black melancholy', 'the melancholy fiend', and 'these black fits' occur at points throughout[10] this is the first time that the figure of the black dog is used to represent it. It is interesting, then, to note that no explanation or context is provided for the usage, and it is not foregrounded in any way; rather, it appears to be part of an already shared language, a phrase Johnson expects Mrs Thrale to understand. It is from this point in the correspondence that the metaphor begins to recur with some regularity. A month later, Mrs Thrale writes from Brighton that:

> ... the black dog shall not make prey of both my master and myself. My master swims now, and forgets the black dog;[11]

to which Johnson replies:

> I shall easily forgive my master his long stay, if he leaves the dog behind him.[12]

The metaphor appears regularly after this point in exchanges between Johnson and Mrs Thrale through 1778 and 1779.[13] In late 1779, the dog appears for the first time in correspondence between Johnson and Boswell, in the form that recurs so notably half a century later in Lockhart's *Memoirs of Sir Walter Scott*, and there is then a substantial gap before what seems to be its final appearance, in a 1783 letter from Johnson to Mrs Thrale. Here, he writes:

> The black Dog I hope always to resist, and in time to drive ... When I rise my breakfast is solitary, the black dog waits to share it, from breakfast to dinner he continues barking ... What shall exclude the black dog from a habitation like this?[14]

From the particular sequence and content of these letters, it seems clear that, among the three correspondents, it is most likely Mrs Thrale with whom the phrase originated. Although the first epistolary use is attributed to Johnson, it is as a term with which he clearly expects Mrs Thrale is to be familiar. Moreover, in the initial occurrences, it is used exclusively to refer to Mr Thrale; although Johnson refers frequently to his own melancholy and low spirits, he does not use the black-dog metaphor with regard to himself until 1783, almost six years after it first appears in the correspondence. In the case of Boswell, it is clear from his journals that it is not a term he himself favours, referring instead to his 'black melancholy' and 'the melancholy fiend', as noted previously.[15] Moreover, a comprehensive study of Boswell's use of the imagery of melancholy makes no reference at all to the metaphorical Black Dog.[16] Finally, the conclusion that the term as used in the correspondence likely stems from Mrs Thrale is also supported by her own observation that:

> The Black Dog is upon his Back; was a common saying some Years ago when a Man was seen troubled with Melancholy: we used to make of it a sort of Byword or Hack Joke here at Streatham ...[17]

Two points are made clear by this statement. Firstly, that in terms of the Thrale–Johnson–Boswell correspondence, the 'Black Dog' seems to have originated from Streatham, from the Thrale household, to which Johnson was a frequent, and Boswell a sometime, visitor. The fact that the first epistolary occurrence of the phrase assumes understanding on the part of the recipient suggests that it may well have been introduced during conversation on one such visit. Secondly, Mrs Thrale's description of a variation on the phrase as being 'a common saying' points to an existing and generalised currency for the usage, which requires that the historian move further back in the quest for origins.

Mrs Thrale herself seems to point the way, telling us in the following passage that:

> Few People however seem to recognize its true Original; which may be found in Dr Henry More's *Philosophical Works*.[18]

Mrs Thrale goes on to cite More's account of Appollonius Tyaneus telling the Greeks that the spirit

> which was the Scourge of the City where he dwelt ... appeared to him in the form of a large *Black Dog*: & leaping *on his Back* sometimes; – filled him with Melancholy for many Days after.[19]

This is certainly a compelling similarity; however Mrs Thrale gives no evidence as to the link between the phrases, or that More was in fact the first to document the use of the saying. The historian would be as ill-advised to accept this conclusion on face-value, as to accept the proclamations of Brewer, or the *OED*, or contemporary belief which associates the phrase with Churchill. The only definitive conclusion to be drawn from Mrs Thrale's claim is that the origins of the phrase lie much earlier, and so the search must continue.

Before we take the next backward step, however, there is an important link to be established, that between Churchill himself and the Black Dog of the Johnson–Boswell–Thrale correspondence. If we are indeed to join the dots to the extent possible, this connection is an important pencil-mark. As Mrs Thrale notes above, the saying was common 'some Years ago', and there is no evidence of its currency during Churchill's time; had there been, his own usage of it would hardly have been as striking as it was. This is the first of our evolutionary gaps: a common usage dies out, and then resurfaces over a century later, rejuvenated by its adoption by a public figure. But is it the same phrase, or a notion Churchill himself came upon independently? It is perhaps not outside the bounds of possibility that what seems a particularly apt metaphor for both the persistence and the darkness of depression might be conceived of independently by one of its sufferers. Nonetheless, there is sufficient evidence to suggest otherwise. Both Johnson and Churchill were famous for their sharp-tongued retorts, and in an essay on Churchill, Anthony Storr notes that he 'was fond of quoting Dr Johnson'.[20] Reviewing a book on Churchill, Richard M Langworth quotes Churchill as having said 'words to the effect that when one is about to be hanged, "it concentrates the mind wonderfully"',[21] and is subsequently taken to task by a reader who notes that the attribution should originally be to Samuel Johnson, citing another Johnson quote often used by Churchill. In response, the journal's editor concedes that 'Churchill had a photographic memory and often ran off his favourite quotes, not always with attribution'.[22] Churchill's familiarity with the work of Samuel Johnson and documented propensity for 'lifting' quotes from that work without citing the source makes it a reasonable assumption that the source of his own usage lies with Johnson, and thereby, with Thrale, and the common saying to which she refers.

Having established the link between Churchill's Black Dog and what Mrs Thrale claims to have been a common-use phrase around the eighteenth century, the task is then to determine the etymology of the phrase itself. If we are to believe Mrs Thrale, the link is via Dr Henry More, to Appollonius Tyaneus in the first century AD. If we are to believe Brewer, the phrase is directly linked to a passage from the Roman poet Horace, whose work dates from around 40 BC, and, interestingly, contemporary translations of Horace's work also seek to make this connection, in a way which can easily mislead the historian without recourse to the original material. In his translation of a key passage from Horace's *Satires II*, John Conington, a Corpus Professor of Latin at Oxford University, cites the character of the slave, Davus, as saying:

Then too you cannot spend an hour alone;
No company's more hateful than your own;

You dodge and give yourself the slip; you seek
In bed or in your cups from care to sneak:
In vain: the black dog follows you, and hangs
Close on your flying skirts with hungry fangs.[23]

Were this a literal translation of the original Latin, it would be a useful breadcrumb indeed. Although there is no direct reference to melancholy or depression in these lines, the picture of a person struggling with himself is clearly drawn; at the same time, there is a telling association of the dog with that internal struggle, what might readily be interpreted as a lyrical representation of melancholy or depression. The 'black dog' metaphor, however, is introduced in the process of translation, rather than being extant in the original manuscript, which reads *comes atra* or, literally, 'black companion'.[24] In an interesting inter-textual red-herring for the historian, Conington's translation maintains the spirit of the original, while introducing the figure of the dog, presumably under the influence of its contemporary currency. While Horace warns that the sight of an actual black dog portends bad luck, and uses the figurative phrase 'black companion' for what seems to be a kind of internal struggle or malaise, he does not directly, as Conington's translation would suggest, make the link between the black dog and the melancholic state.

Also inconvenient for the historian seeking to link either Horace or Appollonius to the contemporary metaphor, is the fact that there is an enormous chronological gap between their writings and the eighteenth century. We have already noted the apparent death of the phrase in the space of a single century before Churchill revived it; how can it be reasonable to assume that it should have, prior to this, endured stolidly across some seventeen hundred years? Despite the associative links that can be made between the two black-dog references, there is no real evidence to suggest a more direct link between the two. Another possible connection may be found in the legend of the Black Dog of Bungay, an account of which was written by a clergyman named Abraham Fleming:

> This black dog, or the divil in such a likenesse … passing by another man of the congregation in the church, gave him such a gripe on the back, that therewith all he was presently drawen togither and shrunk up, as it were a peece of lether scorched in a hot fire …[25]

Notwithstanding doubts in some circles as to whether the author of the leaflet was an actual witness to the event,[26] this version of the Black Dog's visit in 1577 was widely circulated and remains a key aspect of folkloric narrative in Suffolk, a county proximate to Mrs Thrale's home-town of Streatham, in Greater London. This account, in which a devilish black dog physically attacks a man on his back, resulting not in his death, but in him being 'drawen togither and shrunk up', is also reminiscent of the phrase 'the black dog is upon his back' which Mrs Thrale cites as being in common usage two centuries later.

The Black Dog which appears in the Bungay legend is representative of a broader folkloric phenomenon in Britain and Europe at the time. Sightings of devilish black dogs – in a variety of forms and appellations, among them Barghest, Hell Hound, and Whist Hound – were well-documented, and often associated with so-called liminal, or 'border-spaces' between this world and the next, such as graveyards, intersections and ley lines.[27] The creature's appearance was commonly believed to be ominous, to herald some kind of disaster. Theo Brown makes an important distinction in this regard, noting that disaster might be communal or personal, but was usually the latter;[28] that is, popular belief was that a sighting of the Black Dog marked an individual in some way, generating an expectation of personal calamity. It is not difficult to imagine how the internalised sense of foreboding, the pall cast over one's life by such a sighting might translate into a generalised sense of melancholy, again firming the association in the popular imagination between the Black Dog and a depressed state.

As is suggested by the Bungay account, which notes that the Black Dog may be 'the divil in such a likenesse', the association between this creature and the supernatural or otherworldly realm is long-established. This association, which sees the Black Dog appearing as one of the Devil's guises, a witch's familiar, as guardian or gatekeeper of the world of the dead, or as a 'psychopomp', a creature which enables the transition of spirits to that other world, is both cross-cultural and ancient, a staple of Greek, Roman, Egyptian, Middle-Eastern and Norse mythologies.[29] In a contemporary sense, this representation of the Black Dog emerges in literature in forms such as Goethe's Mephistopheles, or Conan Doyle's *Hound of the Baskervilles*.[30] In classical texts, we find the dog in Horace, and in Appollonius, cited by Brewer and Thrale respectively as the likely originators of its use as a metaphor for depression. As I have suggested, however, the menacing connotations which are crucial to these representations of the black dog have much more ancient roots, via their associations with mythological figures such as Hecate, Anubis, and Cerberus. While it is true that the dogs associated with these figures are not necessarily black, they nonetheless establish a relationship between the canine and the underworld to which later representations of the black dog owe a debt.[31]

The question, then, as to how a few lines from Horace and Appollonius could have evolved across so many centuries, persisting until their appearance in the form Mrs Thrale notes, might be answered in a number of ways. Perhaps this did not occur at all. Perhaps the phrase to which she refers comes directly from the incident at Bungay; the link certainly seems a more direct one in many ways. The history of language and symbol, however, is never straightforward. To this point, I have attempted to follow an at-times somewhat tenuous trail of breadcrumbs to examine the history of the Black Dog metaphor, to uncover its point of origin. I would contend, however, that, ultimately, such a point does not exist, and that the evolution of the metaphor is better conceived of as a process of cross-pollination, a circulation of complementary discourses which feed into and inform each other, culminating in the specific image we have today, rather than as a linear process in which a single, identifiable 'original' usage develops and evolves over time. Horace's associations of the black dog with both 'bad luck' and an internal struggle with self may be the first direct references of this kind, but they are predicated on an existing broader discourse which associates the figure of the dog with death and decay. The Black Dog of Bungay makes the direct reference to the Black Dog being on a person's back, which Horace lacks, but there is no explicit reference here to either bad luck or melancholy. The spectral black dogs of British folklore combine associations with the Devil and their ancient positioning as gatekeepers of the Otherworld to act as earthly omens of disaster. Each of these constructions emphasises a different aspect of the creature, and the combination of these operates in an inter-textual process to give the image of the Black Dog the range of associations it has acquired across its long history. To speak of a point of origin becomes moot, since the metaphor as we know it is the sum of all these parts, in complex relationship with each other over time.

To this point, I have referred largely to the Black Dog as a compound phrase, without considering the individual elements of the image. As I mentioned earlier, for a phrase or a symbol to enter common usage, it has to capture the popular imagination, proving itself equal to the task of representing, in this case, melancholy or depression. I have argued that the composite image of the Black Dog itself has been subject to an intertextual process by which a range of different references combine to add weight to its currency; to this, I now add that each part of the image, taken separately, also has a role to play in this process. As Robert Burton notes, the very word 'melancholia' stems in part from the Greek word *melaina*, meaning 'black'.[32] The longstanding symbolic associations of blackness with the supernatural and with negative emotions are indisputable, and as Allan Ingram observes:

> From the earliest writers onwards, melancholy is rarely discussed without attendant images of blackness and obscurity.[33]

Less obvious, perhaps, but no less compelling, are the canine associations with melancholy. Burton contends that of all other animals, dogs are most subject to melancholy

> insomuch as some hold they dream as men do, and through violence of melancholy run mad.[34]

Early medical writers documented a phenomenon they dubbed *melancholia canina*, in which sufferers were observed to go out howling at night,[35] and a number of early texts make explicit associations between the dog and a state of melancholy. The figure of the dog in *Melancolia I*, a sixteenth-century engraving by Albrecht Dürer, has been described as 'a fellow-sufferer with melancolia', and the same scholars cite a range of sources which are unequivocal as to the link between the canine and the melancholic.[36] Of particular relevance to the present investigation is the claim by the eleventh-century Hebrew astrologer Ibn Ezra that the *canes nigri* – or black dog – is the beast of Saturn, the melancholy god.[37] That both key elements in the image have direct associations with depression in their own right adds more inter-textual layers to the image of the Black Dog itself, making its resonance as a metaphor significantly more compelling and multi-dimensional.

The way in which the metaphor has evolved in terms of usage and connotations is reflected in a concomitant evolution in the particular language of the expression. In Horace, 'the black dog follows you and hangs/close on your skirts with hungry fangs'; in Mrs Thrale's common-use phrase, 'the Black Dog is upon his back'; in Brewer, 'a black dog has walked over him'; for Johnson, it was the black dog which 'worried him' and 'continued barking'; for Churchill, it became the 'black dog on [the] shoulder'; and in more contemporary usage, we find it referred to often simply as 'the black dog'. What is visible in this process is a gradual stripping away of the oppressive actions, until only the figure of the dog itself remains, in much the same way that, in Australian culture, the entire complex narrative of the Ned Kelly story has come to be distilled into the iconic armour, into a single, dark eye-hole. Here, the black dog itself comes to be associated with depression, the layers of inter-textual associations that make it such a compelling metaphor rendered largely invisible.

It should be clear, then, that in terms of its historical origins, the Black Dog is not Churchill's, but rather an image whose history likely extends back to classical mythology, and whose endurance in a range of forms owes itself to a plethora of literary, folkloric, psychological, and linguistic factors. The Black Dog is Johnson's and Thrale's and Horace's and Saturn's and many others' besides; there is no single point of origin, no tidy trail of evidence to be followed in a satisfying linear fashion, but rather a complex and untidy multi-layered process of evolution.

I have argued that in a historical sense, the image is not Churchill's, but I would like to conclude by arguing that, in every other sense, it most certainly is. This investigation began with Churchill, and must end with him, because while its central proposition has been to move the Black Dog further and further away from Churchill, to locate its earliest origins, the fact is that it is he who is directly responsible for its contemporary currency.

As previously mentioned, it was Churchill who revived the phrase, almost certainly from his reading of Samuel Johnson. Many others, of course, have read Johnson; many others are familiar with Horace and More and Thrale and the Black Dogs of Britain. But it is because of who Churchill was, and the particular way in which he returned the Black Dog to popular consciousness, that it has evolved into the symbol we have today. He recognised his own suffering in it, and adopted it, and because of his public profile and the unique circumstances of his life, added dimensions to the metaphor that gave it a broader appeal. In association with Churchill, depression becomes something one can struggle with, but not be overcome by, something that can be associated with a figure who is successful and celebrated, a statesman able to inspire a nation. It is a combination of his high profile, and the striking juxtaposition of his public achievements and personal struggle, that have rejuvenated and returned the Black Dog to common parlance as part of the next stage of its evolution. The contemporary Black Dog is in evidence in music, art, literature, and film,[38] taking on a new life of its own, a life prefigured by the myriad of early incarnations discussed in this essay, but which is made possible in its current form, in contemporary culture, only via Churchill's intervention. Historical breadcrumbs aside, the Black Dog we know today is Churchill's, and it is against his own personal history that it takes on its contemporary dimensions, re-configuring depression as something from which one

can separate oneself, something to be named, lived with, tran-
scended. Although history may deny that it is Churchill's Black
Dog, on the most important of levels, it most certainly is.

DREAM AWAY - DAVID FRAZER

Bibliography

Balderston, Katharine C (ed.) 1942, *Thraliana: The Diary of Mrs. Hester
    Lynch Thrale (Later Mrs. Piozzi), 1776–1809*, 2 vols, Clarendon, Oxford.

Baskin, Wade, 1972, *The Dictionary of Satanism*, Philosophical Library.

Bloom, Edward A & Bloom, Lillian D (eds) 1989, *The Piozzi Letters:
    Correspondence of Hester Lynch Piozzi, 1784–1821 (formerly Mrs Thrale)*,
    vol. I, 1784–1791, University of Delaware Press, Newark.

Boswell, James, *Life of Samuel Johnson LL.D.*, vol. 3, 1776–1780 (ed. George
    Birkbeck Hill), accessed online 17 December 2004 at <http://www.full-
    books.com/Life-Of-Johnson-Vol-312.html>.

Brewer, E Cobham, 1898, *Brewer's Dictionary of Phrase and Fable*, Henry
    Altemus, Philadelphia.

Brown, Theo, 1978, 'The black dog in English folklore', in JR Porter &
    WMS Russell (eds), *Animals in Folklore*, Brewer, Cambridge.

Burton, Robert, 1896 (1621), *The Anatomy of Melancholy*, I, George Bell &
    Sons, London.

Chapman, RW (ed.) 1952, *The Letters of Samuel Johnson*, I, 1719–1774; II, 1775–1782; III, 1783–1784, Oxford University Press, London.

Fleming, Abraham, 'A Straunge and Terrible Wunder wrought very late in the parish Church of Bungay', accessed online 15 January 2005 at <http://nli.northampton.a.uk/ass/psych-staff/sjs/Bungay.html>.

Goethe, Johann Wolfgang von, *Faust*, 2nd edn (1909), Macmillan, London.

Harris, Mark (ed.) 1981, *The Heart of Boswell: Six Journals in One Volume*, McGraw-Hill, New York.

Heffernan, Carol Falvo, 'That dog again: "Melancholia Canina and Chaucer's Book of the Duchess"', *Modern Philology*, 84(2), pp. 185–90.

Horace (Q. Horatius Flaccus), *Satires II* (tran. John Conington), available online via Project Gutenberg and accessed on 17 January 2005 at <http://online-books.library.upenn.edu/webbin/gutbook/lookup?num=5419>.

Horace (Q. Horatius Flaccus), *Satires II* (tran. Frances Muecke, 1993), Aris & Phillips, Warminster.

Ingram, Allan, 1982, Boswell's *Creative Gloom: A Study of Imagery and Melancholy in the Writings of James Boswell*, Macmillan, London.

Jenkins, F, 'The role of the dog in Romano–Gaulish religion', *Latomus*, 16, pp. 60–76.

Langworth, Richard M, review of Larry Kryske, 2000, *The Churchill Factors: Creating your Finest Hour*, Trafford, Victoria, in *Finest Hour* no. 110, Spring, 2001, online, accessed 10 December 2004 at <http://www.winstonchurchill.org/i4a/pages/index.cfm?pageid=318>.

Lockhart, JG, 1869, *Memoirs of Sir Walter Scott*, VIII, Black, Edinburgh.

McCarthy, William, 1985, *Hester Thrale Piozzi: Portrait of a Literary Woman*, University of North Carolina Press, Chapel Hill.

The Oxford English Dictionary, 1989, 2nd edn, Clarendon Press, Oxford.

Preston-Day, Leslie, 1984, 'Dog burials in the Greek world', *American Journal of Archaeology*, 88, pp. 21–31.

Piozzi, Hester Lynch, 1974 (1786), *Anecdotes of the Late Samuel Johnson, LL.D*, Garland, New York.

Rowland, Beryl, 1974, *Animals with Human Faces: A Guide to Animal Symbolism*, Allen & Unwin, London.

Sherbo, Arthur, 'Earlier than in OED: The black dog and crap', *Notes and Queries*, 45(2), 186–7.

Stevenson, Robert Louis, 1882, *New Arabian Nights*, Chatto & Windus, London.

Storr, Anthony, 1988, *Churchill's Black Dog, Kafka's Mice, and Other Phenomena of the Human Mind*, Grove Press, New York.

Trubshaw, Bob, 1994, 'Black dogs: Guardians of the corpse ways', *Mercian Mysteries*, 20, August.

Wain, John (ed.) 1991, *The Journals of James Boswell, 1762–1795*, Heinemann, London.

AN OBSERVATION
ABOUT THE INSTITUTE'S
NEW HOME

Visiting the brand new building housing the Black Dog Institute recently, to do some research for this essay, gave me the impression that the stigma associated with mental illness is shifting. In the past (many institutions dedicated to helping the mentally ill) ... were beat up old buildings, tucked away from the rest of the world. The Black Dog Institute's bright orange paintwork and its striking and ingenious logo engenders a sense of warmth, of welcome and of hope. In his recent book *Dealing with Depression*, the Director of the Black Dog Institute, Gordon Parker, writes that depression is the 'common cold of the psyche', and that 25 per cent of women and 20 per cent of men will experience an episode of clinical depression in their lifetime. With such a high incidence, and such a negative history, destigmatising mental illness is important and is in fact one of the Black Dog Institute's commitments.
TERESA

Where to find details about future writing competitions

Information about future Black Dog Institute Writing Competitions can be found on the website <http://www.blackdoginstitute.org.au>.

NOTES

Hairy tales and historical legwork

1   1993, *The Hero with a Thousand Faces*, Fontana Press, London.
2   Ronald Wright, 2005, *A Short History of Progress*, Carroll & Graf.
3   J Serpell, 'From paragon to pariah: some reflections on human attitudes to dogs', quoted in Sophie Menache, 1997, 'Dogs: God's worst enemy?' *Society & Animals Forum*, vol. 5 no. 1.
4   Serpell, 'From paragon to pariah'.
5   Suzanne found the expression in an article by J Idol in *Verbatim*, 7, no. 1, 1980, pp. 9–10.
6   From Chris Schlect, 'Great Hellenic dogs' in *Credenda Agenda* vol. 10 issue 2, accessed from <http://www.credenda.org/issues/10-2historia.php?>.
7   Bob Trubshaw, 'Black dogs: Guardians of the corpse ways', accessed at <http://indigogroup.co.uk/edge/bdogs.htm>.
8   Trubshaw, 'Black dogs'.
9   Book XIII, lines 404–407.
10 From RM Hutchins (ed.) 1952, *Great Books of the Western World*, 10. Hippocrates and Galen, William Benton, Encyclopaedia Britannica Inc., Chicago.
11 *Masters of the Mind*, 2004, Wiley & Sons, New Jersey.
12 RL Tongue, 1965, *Somerset Folklore*, vol. VIII, The Folk-Lore Society, London.
13 Trubshaw, 'Black dogs'.
14 K Silverman, 1983, *From Sign to Subject: The Subject of Semiotics*, Oxford University Press, Oxford.
15 1984, Cornell University Press, Ithaca, NY.
16 2000, New Harbinger Publications, Oakland, CA.
17 Michael McDonald, 1981, *Mystical Bedlam*, Cambridge University Press.
18 BG Walker, 1983, *The Women's Encyclopaedia of Myths and Secrets*, HarperCollins, New York.

19 J Bord & C Bord, 1980, *Alien Animals: A Worldwide Investigation*, Granada, London; Fortean Picture Library, Henblas, Mwrog Street, Ruthin, LL15 1LG, UK.

20 Walker, *The Women's Encyclopaedia of Myths and Secrets*.

21 From <http://www.malleusmaleficarum.org>.

22 From <http://www.hulford.co.uk/ergot.html>.

23 R Cavendish (ed.) 1955, *The Illustrated Encyclopaedia of Mythology, Religion and the Unknown*, Marshall Cavendish, New York.

24 From <http://www.skell.org/explore/text/medT.html>.

25 JC Cooper, 1978, *An Illustrated Encyclopaedia of Traditional Symbols*, Thames & Hudson, London.

26 Quoted in C Heffernan, 'That dog again: Melancholia canina', *Modern Philology*, vol. 84, no. 2, pp. 185–90.

27 From <http://nli.northampton.ac.uk/ass/psych-staff/sjs/Bungay.htm>.

28 Bord & Bord, *Alien Animals;* Fortean Picture Library.

29 T Bullfinch, 1964, *Bullfinch's Complete Mythology*, Hamlin, London.

30 T Bullfinch, 'The Age of Chivalry', accessed at <http://www.bartleby.com/182/101.html>.

31 MA Screech, 2000, *Montaigne and Melancholy: The Wisdom of the Essays*, Duckworth, London.

32 Web Dictionary of the History of Ideas, <http://etext.lib.virginia.edu/cgi-local/DHI/dhi.cgi?id=dv3-33>.

33 From <http://www.vanderbilt.edu/htdocs/Blair/Courses/MUSL242/f98/mluther.htm>.

34 Web Dictionary of the History of Ideas.

35 Citing Maurice Palmer Tilley, 1950, *A Dictionary of the Proverbs in England in the Sixteenth and Seventeenth Century*, UMP, Ann Arbor.

36 Robert Burton, 1979 (1621), *The Anatomy of Melancholy*, abr. & ed. J & K Peters, Frederick Unger, New York.

37 From http://en.wikipedia.org/wiki/JohannWeyer.

38 R Porter (ed.) 1982, *Mood Disorders*, University of Pittsburgh Press, Pittsburgh.

39 From Michel Foucault, 1965, *Madness and Civilization: A History of Insanity in the Age of Reason*, trans. R Howard, Tavistock. London.

40 Porter, *Mood Disorders*.

41 A Solomon, 2001, *The Noonday Demon: An Atlas of Depression*, Scribner, New York.

42 GB Harrison, 1929, 'On Elizabethan melancholy' in Nicholas Breton, *Melancholike Humours*, Scholartis Press, London.

43 Lawrence Babb, 1951, *The Elizabethan Malady: A Study of Melancholia in English Literature from 1580 to 1642*, Michigan State College Press, East Lansing.

44 From <http://shadowlight.gydja.com/melancholy.html>.

45 2002, Chatto & Windus, London.

46 Susan Agrawal, abstract of a paper entitled 'Imitations of melancholic and sanguine humoural symptoms in the music of the English ayre', accessed at <http://www.princeton.edu/~rwegman/abstract.htm>.

47 Viking Press, New York, 1972.

48 Joseph M Ortiz, abstract of a paper entitled '*Sine ore loquens*: Melancholy and incorporeal music in early modern England', accessed at <http://www.princeton.edu/~rwegman/abstract.htm>.

49 In WF Bynum, R Porter & M Shepherd (eds) 1985, *The Anatomy of Madness*, Tavistock, London.

50 J Boswell, 1953 (1791), *The Life of Samuel Johnson*, Oxford University Press, London.

51 2002, Carroll & Graf, New York.

52 'The Journal of Sir Walter Scott', 1970 (1890), Burt Franklin, New York, accessed at <http://www.gutenberg.org/files/14860/14860-h/vol_ii.html>.

53 Solomon, *The Noonday Demon*.

54 1981 (1969), Blackwell, Oxford.

55 From <http://www.themystica.com/mystica/articles/m/mesmerism.html>.

56 1872, *Traditions, Superstitions, and Folk-Lore*, Ireland & Co, Manchester,.

57 1988, *Spirits, Fairies, Gnomes and Goblins: An Encyclopaedia of the Little People*, ABC-CLIO, Oxford.

58 Accessed at <http://etext.library.adelaide.edu.au/m/mill/john_stuart/m645a/auto05.htm>.

59 From <http://www.castleofspirits.com/blackdogs2.htm>.

60 1997, *Killing the Black Dog: Essays and Poems*, Federation Press, Sydney.

61 From <http://www.writewords.org.uk>.

62 Anthony Storr, 1988, *Churchill's Black Dog, Kafka's Mice and Other Phenomena of the Human Mind*, Grove Press, New York.

63 Sue Chance, 'Chance Thoughts', *Continuing Medical Education*, Jan 1996, accessed from <http://www.mhsource.com/exclusive/chanceth0196.html>.

64 From 'My life with my parents, Winston and Clementine', accessed at <http://www.winstonchurchill.org/i4a/pages/index.cfm?pageid=775>.

65 From <http://en.wikipedia.org/wiki/Black_Shuck>.

66 Jonathan Cape, London.

67 1979, Virago, London.

68 JC Cooper, 1978, *An Illustrated Encyclopaedia of Traditional Symbols*, Thames Hudson, London.

69 1992, Vintage Press, London.

'Black dog' as a metaphor for depression: A brief history

1   *Black dog*. Words and music by Chris O'Doherty © Syray Music/Universal Music Publishing P/L. Reprinted with permission. All rights reserved.

2   SR Adler, 1991, 'Sudden Unexpected Nocturnal Death Syndrome among Hmong immigrants: Examining the role of the "nightmare"', *Journal of American Folklore* 104: pp. 54–71.

3   J Colville, 'The personality of Sir Winston Churchill' (Crosby Kemper Lecture, 24 March 1985) in RC Kemper (ed.) 1995, *Winston Churchill: Resolution, Defiance, Magnanimity, Good Will*, University of Missouri, Columbia, pp. 108–25. See also M Gilbert, 1994, *In Search of Churchill: A Historian's Journey*, Harper Collins, London, pp. 209ff.

4   JA Murray et al. (eds) 1888, *A New English Dictionary on Historical Principles*, vol. I/2, Clarendon, Oxford, p. 892. This definition is retained unchanged by the current edition of the *OED*.

5   RE Cole, 1886, *Glossary of Words Used in South-West Lincolnshire*, English Dialect Society, London, cited in TB Haber, 1965, 'Canine terms applied to human beings and human events', *American Speech* 40, p. 91.

6   JS Farmer & WE Henley, 1890, *Slang and its Analogues, Past and Present*, vol. I, private print, London, p. 212.

7   JS Farmer, 1905, *A Dictionary of Slang and Colloquial English* (abridged from the seven-volume *Slang and its Analogues, Past and Present*), Routledge, London, p. 48.

8   J Wright (ed.) 1898–1905, *The English Dialect Dictionary: Being the Complete Vocabulary of All Dialect Words Still in Use, or Known to have been in Use During the Last Two Hundred Years*, Oxford University, London, p. 280.

9   WD Whitney (ed.) 1889, *The Century Dictionary: An Encyclopaedia Lexicon of the English Language*, vol. I, Century, New York, p. 572.

10   R Chambers (ed.) 1864, *The Book of Days: A Miscellany of Popular Antiquities in Connection with the Calendar*, Chambers, London, p. 433.

11   Wright, *The English Dialect Dictionary*, p. 150; entry for 'monkey' (n) (definitions 24 and 33) in current *OED*.

12   EC Brewer, 1894, *Dictionary of Phrase and Fable* (new, enlarged edn), Cassell, London, p. 365.

13   In the seventeenth century, it was reported that a 'Bitch with whelps, a Fixon with cubs' were also evil omens in Athens, and that a black dog entering the house was inauspicious, but the information appears to derive from Roman sources; F Rous, 1654, *Archæologiæ Atticæ*, 4th ed., John Adams & Ed Forrest, Oxford, pp. 74, 369; A Sammes, 1676, *Britannia Antiqua Illustrate, or, The Antiquities of Ancient Britain*, the

author, London, p. 366; J Potter, 1697, *Archæologiæ Græcæ, or, The Antiquities of Greece*, A Swall, Oxford, p. 130.

14 J Conington (tran.) 1863, *The Satires, Epistles, and Art of Poetry of Horace*, George Bell & Sons, London, p. 90.

15 C Smart, 1767, *The Works of Horace Translated into Verse, with a Prose Interpretation for the Use of Students*, vol. 3, W Flexney, Messrs. Johnson & Co & T Caslon, London, p. 277. The verse translation was: 'for sticking to your back/he is your constant friend in black'.

16 F Orth, 1913, 'Hund', in AF von Pauly (ed.) 1894–1980, *Realencyclopädie der classischen Altertumswissenschaft*, vol. 8, JB Metzler, Stuttgart, col. 2578.

17 C Hünemörder, 1998, 'Hund', in H Cancik & H Schneider (eds) 1996–2003, *Der neue Pauly: Enzyklopädie der Antike*, vol. 5, Metzler, Stuttgart, col. 757.

18 EE Burriss, 1935, 'The place of the dog in superstition as revealed in Latin literature', *Classical Philology* 30, pp. 32–42.

19 F Jenkins, 1957, 'The role of the dog in Romano-Gaulish religion', *Latomus* 16, pp. 60–76; JMC Toynbee, 1973, *Animals in Roman Life and Art*, Cornell University. Ithaca, pp. 122f.

20 See Orth, 'Hund'; Toynbee, *Animals in Roman Life and Art*.

21 For example, Galen's 'On Melancholy' in CG Kuhn (ed., tran.) 1821–33, *Claudii Galeni Opera Omnia* (reprinted Olms, Hildesheim, 1964–65), vol. XIX, p. 719.

22 E Panofsky & F Saxl, 1923, *Dürer's 'Melencolia I': Eine quellen- und typengeschichtliche Untersuchung*, Teubner, Leipzig.

23 G Jászai, 1991, 'Hunde', in R Auty et al. (eds) 1977–98, *Lexikon des Mittelalters*, vol. 5, Artemis, Munich, col. 213f.; P Gerlach, 1970, 'Hund' in E Kirschbaum (ed.) 1968–76, *Lexikon der christlichen Ikonographie*, vol. II, Herder, Rome, col. 334–6.

24 IH Evans (ed.) 1970, *Brewer's Dictionary of Phrase & Fable*, centenary edn, Cassell, London, p. 329.

25 These and further examples in MP Tilley, 1950, *A Dictionary of Proverbs in England in the Sixteenth and Seventeenth Centuries*, University of Michigan, Ann Arbor, p. 163.

26 Democritus Junior (= R Burton) 1621, *The Anatomy of Melancholy*. I have cited the 16th edition (P Blake, London, 1836), based on the authorised 1651 edition, as the spelling is more familiar to modern readers: preface, p.44.

27 Part 1, sect. 3, mem. 1, subsect. 2 (1621, p. 233; 1836, p. 254).

28 Part 3, sect. 4, mem. 2, subsect. 6 (not in 1621 edn; 1836, p. 733).

29 Part 3, sect. 4, mem. 2, subsect. 4 (1621, p. 781; 1836, p. 722).

30 N Wanley, 1678, *The Wonders of the Little World, or, A General History of*

Man, T Basset, R Cheswel, J Wright & T Sawbridge, London, p. 611; R Burton (= N Crouch) 1729, *Wonderful Prodigies of Judgment and Mercy Discovered in Near Three Hundred Memorable Histories*, A Bettesworth & J Batley, London, p. 62; Artemidorus, *The Interpretation of Dreams: First written in Greek… and now made into English*, J Bew, London, 1755, p. 156.

31 'Mr Village to Mr Town', *The Connoisseur*, 13 March 1755, pp. 109–12.

32 *Titus Andronicus*, Act V, scene 1; Aaron is a Moor. 'To blush like a black (or blue) dog' (that is, not at all) was current from at least the end of the sixteenth century until the nineteenth century: see also Farmer, *A Dictionary of Slang and Colloquial English*.

33 T Duffett, 1678, *Psyche Debauch'd*, John Smith, London, p. 60.

34 HL Piozzi (ed.) 1788, *Letters to and from the Late Samuel Johnson, LL.D*, vol. 1, A Strahan & T Cadell, London, p. 331.

35 Piozzi, *Letters*, vol. 2, p. 26.

36 Piozzi, *Letters*, vol. 2, p. 32f. (11 November 1778).

37 Piozzi, *Letters*, vol. 2, p. 37 (14 November 1778).

38 S Johnson, 1892, *Letters of Samuel Johnson*, collected and edited by GB Hill, Clarendon, Oxford, no. 592 (21 November 1778).

39 Piozzi, *Letters*, vol. 2, p. 280f. (28 June 1783).

40 J Boswell, 1887, *The life of Samuel Johnson LL.D*, vol. 3, 3rd edn (ed. GB Hill), Clarendon, Oxford, p. 414 (October 27 1779). The Burton citation is from the final lines of *The Anatomy of Melancholy*.

41 Boswell, *Life of Johnson*, vol. 3, p. 416.

42 His dictionary did, however, include among the definitions for 'dog': 'a reproachful term for a man', in which sense Johnson also employed 'black dog': see Boswell, *Life of Johnson*, vol.1, p. 284.

43 KC Balderston (ed.) 1942, *Thraliana: The Diary of Mrs. Hester Lynch Thrale (later Mrs. Piozzi), 1776–1809*, Clarendon, Oxford, p. 785.

44 Balderston, *Thraliana*; H More, 1660, *Explanation of the Grand Mystery of Godliness*, W Morden, London: *Apollonius in Ephesus*, p. 121.

45 H More, 1662, *A Collection of Several Philosophical Writings*, W Morden, London.

46 H More, 'Antidote against Atheism' in *A Collection of Several Philosophical Writings*, vol. 1, p. 125; Philostratus' account is found at IV, 10 (vol. 1, pp. 362–7 of the Loeb edition: William Heinemann, London, 1912).

47 H More, 'Enthusiasmus Triumphatus; or, A Brief Discourse on the Nature, Causes, Kinds, and Cure of Enthusiasm' in *A Collection of Several Philosophical Writings*, vol. 1, pp. 8–17; see also J Wier, 1563, *De praestigiis daemonum, et incantationibus, ac veneficiis*, Oporin, Basel.

48 H More, 1656, *Enthusiasmus Triumphatus, or, A Discourse of the Nature,*

Causes, Kinds, and Cure, of Enthusiasme, W Morden, London, p. 179.

49 R Baxter, 1691, *The Certainty of the Worlds of Spirits and, Consequently, of the Immortality of Souls*, T Parkhurst & J Salisbury, London, pp. 193–4; see also pp. 152–4. There were many 'wonder' reports in which the appearance of a black dog presaged misfortune, especially mental illness; for example, I Goulart, 1607, *Admirable and Memorable Histories Containing the Wonders of our Time...* (tran. E Grimeston), George Eld, London, pp. 176–9.

50 L Urdang (ed.) 1985, *Picturesque Expressions: A Thematic Dictionary*, 2nd edn, Gale Research, Detroit, p. 176 (87.1: 'Dejection').

51 Balderston, *Thraliana*, p. 870 (18 February 1794).

52 See, for example, H Schipperges, 1967, 'Melancolia als ein mittelalterlich-er Sammelbegriff für Wahnvorstellungen', in *Studium generale*, Berlin, 20: pp. 723–36. For an exemplary case study of major depression in the ancient world (Cicero), see K Evans, 2000, *Representations of Mental Illness in the Classical Texts*, thesis, University of Queensland, pp. 138–61.

53 T Willis, 1676, *De anima brutorum, quae hominis vitalis ac sensitiva est ...* Huguetan, London, par 2, cap. xi (p. 238).

54 GB Hill, 1897, *Johnsonian Miscellanies*, vol. 1, Clarendon, Oxford, p. 26 (Easter 1761). See also Boswell, *Life of Johnson*, vol. 1, p. 297 (after the completion of his dictionary in 1755, Johnson's mind was 'in such a state of depression'). 'Depression' referred generally to any decline in physiological capacity.

55 SW Jackson, 1981, 'Acedia: The sin and its relationship to sorrow and melancholia in medieval times', *Bulletin of the History of Medicine*, 55: 172–81.

56 John Milton, 1638, *Il penseroso* = the 'thoughtful', 'pensive'.

57 GMA Baretti, 1790, *A Dictionary of the English and Italian Languages ... Corrected and Improved*, JF & C Rivington, London. A similar defi-nition was listed for 'To have a dog in one's belly', which, unlike 'black dog', also appeared in the 1760 edition.

58 F Grose, 1788, *A Classical Dictionary of the Vulgar Tongue*, 2nd edn, Hooper & Wigstead, London.

59 W Scott, 1893, *The Antiquary*, vol. I, John C Nimmo, London, p. 79.

60 JG Lockhart, 1839, *Memoirs of the Life of Sir Walter Scott*, vol. 8, 2nd edn, Robert Cadell, Edinburgh, p. 335; T Carlyle, 1908, 'Sir Walter Scott' in *Sartor Resartus and Essays on Burns and Scott*, Cassell, London, p. 338.

61 RL Stevenson, 1923, 'A lodging for the night', in *New Arabian Nights*, Heinemann, London, p. 223.

62 TB Haber, 1965, 'Canine terms applied to human beings and human events', *American Speech* 40, pp. 83–101; 243–71.

63 AF Moe, 1969, 'On Haber's "Canine terms applied to human beings and human events"', *American Speech* 44: pp. 33–54.

64 RL Stevenson, 1911, *Works*, vol. II, part 1, chapter 2, Chatto & Windus, London, p. 20.

65 JB Cabell, 1923, *Jurgen: A Comedy of Justice*, ch. 38, McBride & Co, New York, p. 243.

66 For example, SW Jackson, 1986, *Melancholia and Depression: From Hippocratic Times to Modern Times*, Yale University, New Haven, pp. 395–9. Nor, surprisingly, is it included in RA Palmatier, 1995, *Speaking of Animals: A Dictionary of Animal Metaphors*, Greenwood, Westport.

67 Churchill, incidentally, is said to have had his childhood labrador taxidermically prepared.

68 C Jürgens, 1999, *Er liebt sie, liebt sie nicht*, Die Zeit, Hamburg, nr.13.

69 JC Chevalier, 1969, *Dictionnaire des Symboles: Mythes, Rêves, Coutumes* ..., Laffont, Paris, p. 199.

70 P Pinel, 1809, *Traité Médico-Philosophique sur L'aliénation Mentale*, JA Brosson, Paris, pp. 104f., §119.

71 Pinel, *Traité Médico-Philosophique*, pp. 168f., §166.

72 J Addison, 1712, *The Spectator*, Saturday May 24, in H Morley (ed.) 1888, *The Spectator: A New Edition, Reproducing the Original Text* ..., Routledge, London, p. 564.

73 G Cheyne, 1734, *The English Malady: or, a Treatise of Nervous Diseases of All Kinds; as Spleen, Vapours, Lowness of Spirits, Hypochondriacal, and Hysterical Distempers, etc.*, Strahan, London, opening lines.

74 For literature, see J Bord & C Bord, 1980, *Alien Animals: A Worldwide Investigation*, Granada, London; J Simpson & S Roud, 2001, *A Dictionary of English Folklore*, Oxford University, Oxford; B Trubshaw, 1994/2001, 'Black dogs in folklore', <http://www.indigogroup.co.uk/edge/bdogfl.htm>, viewed 20 January 2005; J Harte, 1998, *Alternative Approaches to Folklore: A Bibliography 1969–1996*, Heart of Albion, Loughborough.

75 Contributed by WH Miller (hojo2x@aol.com) to newsgroup rec.music.makers.guitar.acoustic, 3 July 1999; thread Re: Catharsis (may be long).

76 Chambers, *The Book of Days*.

77 For example, Farmer & Henley, *Slang and its Analogues, Past and Present*: '(common) delirium tremens, the horrors, "jim jams"'.

78 For example, T Hughes, 1861, *Tom Brown at Oxford*: 'D.T., sir. After one of his rages the 'black dog' comes, and its hawful work ...', ch. xxxi ii; in undated reprint, Thomas Nelson, London, p. 391.

79 LV Berrey & M Van den Bark, 1942, *The American Thesaurus of Slang*, Thomas Y Crowell, New York; pp. 157 (130.9: 'delirium tremens'), 290f.

(283.2-7: 'sullenness'). 'Les papillon noirs' was apparently employed in France for both delirium tremens and hypochondria: Farmer & Henley, *Slang and its Analogues, Past and Present*, vol. III, p.105.

80 This (from Ngaio Marsh, 1949, *A Wreath for Rivera*), and other examples, 1932–76, in BJ Whiting, 1989, *Modern Proverbs and Proverbial Sayings*, Harvard University, Cambridge, p. 178.

81 'To have a black dog on the shoulder': LK Henderson, 1956, *Dictionary of English Idioms*, vol. II, J Blackwood, London, p.71.

82 See entries in *OED* for 'blues' and 'blue devils'.

83 J Green, 2000, *Cassell's Dictionary of Slang*, Cassell, London, p. 100. This volume also lists 'black rot' as a nineteenth century American expression for intense depression: p. 102.

84 E Partridge, 1961, *A Dictionary of Slang and Unconventional English* ..., 5th edn, repr. 1970, Routledge & Kegan Paul, London, p. 59; also in E Partridge, 1972, *A Dictionary Of Historical Slang*, abr. J Simpson from Partridge, 1961, Penguin, Harmondsworth, p. 77. Partridge cited TRG Lyell, 1931, *Slang, Phrase, and Idiom in Colloquial English and their Use*, Hokuseido Press, Tokyo, as his source. Strangely, E Partridge, 1973, *The Routledge Dictionary of Historical Slang*, Routledge & Kegan Paul, London, also described as the abridgement by Simpson of Partridge's 1961 work, records on p. 77 that the term dates from 1825, citing Scott as source.

85 Partridge, *The Routledge Dictionary of Historical Slang*, p. 711. Apart from the fact that 'pompey' was dialectic in parts of England for 'small boy' or 'imp', I have not been able to further track this expression.

86 For example, Les Murray, 1997, *Killing the Black Dog*, Federation Press, Annandale; poems dealing with his handling of depression.

87 Bob Dylan, 1966, *Obviously Five Believers* – 'I got my black dog barking ...'; Jesse Winchester, 1971, *Black Dog*; Nick Drake, 1974, *Black-Eyed Dog*; Mental as Anything, 1998, *Black Dog*.

88 *Black dog*. Words and music by Chris O'Doherty © Syray Music/Universal Music Publishing P/L. Reprinted with permission. All rights reserved.

Black bile and man's best friend: A history of the Black Dog

1 W Meyer & M Pakur, 1999, 'Thoughts about the domestic dog as the catalyst for relations between humans and a body contact object for humans', *Schweiz Arch Tierheilkd* 141(8), pp. 351–9.

2 Horace, *The Odes of Horace* (tran. James Michie, 1970) Penguin, Harmondsworth. pp. 194–5.

3 Johann Wolfgang von Goethe, 1985 (?) *Faust* (tran. John Anster) Harrap, London, p. 68.

4 Robert Burton, 1927 (1621), *The Anatomy of Melancholy* (eds Floyd Dell & Paul Jordan-Smith), Tudor Publishing Company, New York, p. 328.

5 Horace, *Satires, Epistles and Ars Poetica*, (tran. H Rushton Fairclough, 1999), Harvard University Press, Cambridge, p. 234.

6 Horace, *The Satires, Epistles and Art of Poetry of Horace* (tran. John Conington, 1902) George Bell, London, p. 102.

7 Horace, *Satires, Epistles and Ars Poetica*, p. 235.

8 Horace, *The Odes of Horace*, pp. 138–9.

9 Horace, *The Odes of Horace*, p. 241.

10 Aristotle, *The Physics*, vol. 1 (tran. Philip H Wicksteed & Francis M Cornford, 1929), Heinemann, London. pp. 51–7.

11 Hippocrates, *The Genuine Works of Hippocrates*, vol. 1 (tran. Francis Adams, 1849), The Sydenham Society, London, p. 161ff.

12 Timothy Bright, 1940 (1586), *A Treatise of Melancholie*, Facsimile Text Society, New York, p. 102. Bright's *Treatise* was an important source for Burton's *Anatomy*.

13 Burton, *The Anatomy of Melancholy*, p. 169.

14 James Boswell, 1934 (1791) *Life of Samuel Johnson*, LL.D., vol. 2, (ed. George Birkbeck Hill, revised LF Powell), Clarendon Press, Oxford, p. 121.

15 Letter 857 to Mrs Thrale, June 28 1783, Samuel Johnson, *Letters of Samuel Johnson*, vol. 2, Jan. 15 1777–Dec. 18 1784 (ed. George Birkbeck Hill, 1892), Clarendon, Oxford, p. 309.

16 Letter 586 to Mrs Thrale, October 31 1778, Johnson, *Letters*, p. 73.

17 Cited in Johnson, *Letters*, p. 73.

18 Letter 591 to Mrs Thrale, November 14 1778, Johnson, *Letters*, p. 76.

19 Letter 591 to Mrs Thrale, November 14 1778, Johnson, *Letters*, p. 76.

20 Letter 592 to Mrs Thrale, November 28 1778, Johnson, *Letters*, p. 79.

21 Boswell, *Life of Johnson*. p. 414.

22 Hester Thrale, *Thraliana: The Diary of Mrs Hester Lynch Thrale (Later Mrs Piozzi) 1776–1809*, vol. 2, 1784–1809 (ed. Katharine C Balderston, 1942) Clarendon, Oxford, p. 784.

23 Thrale, *Thraliana*, p. 870. The anecdote is not quite so detailed in Burton: 'Cardinal Crescence died so likewise desparate [as Francis Spira, an Advocate of Padua] at Verona, still he thought a black dog followed him to his death-bed, no man could drive the dog away.'" Burton, *Anatomy of Melancholy*, p. 984.

24 see Merriam-Webster Online: <http://www.merriam-webster.com/cgi-bin/wftwarch.pl?100704>.

25 Thrale, *Thraliana*, p. 870 no 2.

26 Robert Chambers, 1879, *Book of Days: A Miscellany of Popular Antiquities in Connection with the Calendar*, vol. 2, J.B Lippincott & Co, Philadelphia, p. 433.

27 Chambers, *Book of Days*, p. 433.
28 Chambers, *Book of Days*, p. 433.
29 Chambers, *Book of Days*, p. 434.
30 Lord Moran, *Winston Churchill: The Struggle for Survival 1940–1965*, Constable, London, 1966, p. 181.
31 From CNN, *Larry King Live*: 'Interview with panel of doctors who performed surgery on former President Clinton', September 6, 2004: KING: Dr. Smith, a very common post-operative concept is some sort of depression, mild depression, sometimes serious. Have you found that to be true, and do you tell the president about it, to expect it? SMITH: I have found that to be true, and we did specifically discuss this with him, partly because we often do, but also because he actually raised the question. It is common. It is rarely anything that is not self-limited. I would have a hard time thinking of a patient who required real psychiatric treatment for typical post-operative depression. And we did talk about it a bit. KING: But you do get – I remember the weeps. You do get moments of really being down, maybe because, of course, it's your heart? SMITH: I'm not sure entirely what's behind it, but that is definitely very common. I think we see this in 30 to 40 per cent of the patients we operate on to some degree.

Churchill's black dog? The history of the Black Dog as a metaphor for depression

1   Greg Arnold, 1993, 'Churchill's Black Dog'. Robert Carter's poem 'Black Dog' also begins, 'Bitten by Churchill's black dog…' (*Southerly*, 54(1)).
2. *Oxford English Dictionary*, s.v. black dog, 2.
3   1882, Chatto & Windus, London, p. 111.
4   Stevenson, *New Arabian Nights*, p. 111.
5   JG Lockhart, 1869, *Memoirs of Sir Walter Scott*, VIII, Black, Edinburgh, p. 335.
6   RW Chapman (ed.) 1952, *The Letters of Samuel Johnson*, II, 1775–82, Oxford University Press, London, p. 314 (italics in original).
7   E Cobham Brewer, 1898, *Brewer's Dictionary of Phrase and Fable*, Henry Altemus Company, Philadelphia, 'dog', 8.
8   As cited in Wade Baskin, 1972, *The Dictionary of Satanism*, Philosophical Library, p. 111.
9   Chapman, *Letters*, II, p. 262.
10 See, for example, Chapman, *Letters*, II, pp. 82, 145; John Wain (ed.) 1991, *The Journals of James Boswell, 1762–1795*, Heinemann, London, pp. 92, 93.

11 Cited in James Boswell, *Life of Samuel Johnson LL.D.*, vol. 3, 1776–1780 (ed. George Birkbeck Hill), accessed online 17 December 2004 at <http://www.fullbooks.com/Life-Of-Johnson-Vol-312.html>.

12 Chapman, *Letters*, II, p. 268.

13 See, for example, correspondence in November, 1778; March, 1779; June 1779 (Chapman, *Letters*, II, pp. 270, 281, 290).

14 RW Chapman (ed.) 1952, *The Letters of Samuel Johnson*, III, 1783–1784, Oxford University Press, London, p. 41.

15 *The Journals of James Boswell*, pp. 92, 93.

16 See Allan Ingram, 1982, *Boswell's Creative Gloom: A Study of Imagery and Melancholy in the Writings of James Boswell*, Macmillan, London.

17 Katharine C Balderston (ed.) 1942, *Thraliana: The Diary of Mrs. Hester Lynch Thrale (Later Mrs. Piozzi), 1776–1809*, 2 vols, Clarendon, Oxford, p. 785, cited in Arthur Sherbo, 'Earlier than in OED: The black dog and crap', *Notes and Queries*, 45(2), pp. 186–7.

18 Balderston, *Thraliana*, p. 785.

19 Balderston, *Thraliana*, p. 785.

20 Anthony Storr, 1988, *Churchill's Black Dog, Kafka's Mice, and Other Phenomena of the Human Mind*, Grove Press, New York, p. 38.

21 Review of Larry Kryske, *The Churchill Factors: Creating Your Finest Hour*, Trafford, Victoria 2000), in *Finest Hour* no. 110, Spring, 2001, online, accessed 10 December 2004 at <http://www.winstonchurchill.org/i4a/pages/index.cfm?pageid=318>.

22 The exchange takes place online at <http://www.winstonchurchill.org/i4a/pages/index.cfm?pageid=288>, accessed 10 December 2004.

23 Q. Horatius Flaccus, *Satires II* (trans John Conington), available online via Project Gutenberg and accessed 17 January 2005 at <http://online-books.library.upenn.edu/webbin/gutbook/lookup?num=5419>.

24 Q. Horatius Flaccus, *Satires II*, VII, (intr. and tran. Frances Muecke, 1993), Aris & Phillips, Warminster, line 166.

25 Abraham Fleming, 'A Straunge and Terrible Wunder wrought very late in the parish Church of Bungay', excerpt online accessed 15 January 2005 at <http://nli.northampton.a.uk/ass/psych-staff/sjs/Bungay.htm>.

26 See <http://nli.northampton.ac.uk/ass/psych-staff/sjs/Bungay.htm>, accessed 15 January 2005.

27 For a discussion of this issue, see Theo Brown, 'The black dog in English folklore', in JR Porter and WMS Russell (eds) 1978, *Animals in Folklore*, Brewer, Cambridge, pp. 45–58. A ley line is defined as a kind of energy channel in the nervous system of the earth; it was believed that spirits used to travel along these ancient paths.

28 'The Black Dog in English Folklore', p. 57.

29 For a discussion of this issue see, for example, Brown, 'The black dog

in English folklore'; Bob Trubshaw, 1994, 'Black dogs: Guardians of the corpse ways', *Mercian Mysteries*, 20, August; Leslie Preston-Day, 1984, 'Dog burials in the Greek world', *American Journal of Archaeology*, 88, pp. 21–31; and F. Jenkins, 'The role of the dog in Romano-Gaulish religion', *Latomus*, 16, pp. 60–76.

30 Johann Wolfgang von Goethe, *Faust*, Part I, Scene 2, 2nd edn (1909), Macmillan, London.

31 For a discussion of the relationship between these classical dog-figures and the spectral Black Dogs of British folklore, see, for example, Brown, 'The black dog in English folklore', and Trubshaw, 'Black dogs: Guardians of the corpse ways'.

32 Robert Burton, *The Anatomy of Melancholy*, I, George Bell & Sons, London, 1896, p. 193.

33 Ingram, *Boswell's Creative Gloom*, p. 15.

34 Burton, *The Anatomy of Melancholy*, I, p. 87.

35 Carol Falvo Heffernan, 'That dog again: "Melancholia Canina and Chaucer's Book of the Duchess", *Modern Philology*, 84(2), pp. 185–90 (p.188).

36 Cited in Heffernan, p. 189.

37 Cited in Heffernan, p. 190.

38 In the music of bands such as Led Zeppelin (*Black Dog*), The Manic Street Preachers (*Black Dog on My Shoulder*) and Things of Stone and Wood (*Churchill's Black Dog*); the poetry of Les Murray, who devoted a collection containing an essay and a series of poems to his own struggle with depression (*Killing the Black Dog*, The Federation Press, Sydney, 1997); the film *Black Dog* (dir. Lou Birks, UK, BBC, 1999); and recent fiction and memoir by writers such as Ian McEwan (*Black Dogs*, Doubleday, New York, 1992) and John Bentley Mays (*In the Jaws of the Black Dog*, Penguin, London, 1993), among many others.